D0889649

BASS FISHING

In North Carolina
Second Edition

For
DORIS DALE
still my best catch
and
CONRAD and JOHN GERARD
my sons and good fishing partners

Buck Paysour

BASS FISHING

In North Carolina
Second Edition

ISBN 0-929307-03-8

MANUFACTURED IN THE UNITED STATES OF AMERICA

1 2 3 4 5 6 7 8 9

SECOND EDITION, FIRST PRINTING

Table Of Contents

Table of Contents

Foreword

STATE OF NORTH CAROLINA
OFFICE OF THE GOVERNOR
RALEIGH 27611

JAMES G. MARTIN   September 7, 1988
GOVERNOR

Dear Buck:

I am honored and pleased to offer a few introductory comments
to your new edition of "Bass Fishing in North Carolina." Few
books have been in such great demand and such short supply as
yours. Like many other North Carolina anglers, I have eagerly
awaited this book.

In May, 1983, when I was a United States Congressman from
the Ninth District, my youngest son, Ben, and I enjoyed your
practical advice and straightforward reporting. In fact, the
reading was so enjoyable and the advice so helpful that we put
together a stringer full of bass from the Currituck Sound! Your
book proved particularly helpful to us during that father-son
venture into the waters of Northeastern North Carolina. Ben took
his limit of largemouth both days with a Johnson spoon, and I
was only slightly off the pace with a fly rod.

"Bass Fishing in North Carolina" is now a well worn member
of my personal library. It has comforted me on cold winter
evenings and helped me prepare for those precious moments when
I could get away to cast a few old plugs along our rocky Lake
Norman shore.

North Carolina's blessings are plentiful for those of us
who enjoy fishing. And "Bass Fishing in North Carolina" has become
almost as much a part of our fishing heritage in North Carolina
as the bass itself. All of us in this State owe you a debt of
personal thanks for your first book ... and now, finally, the
long-awaited second edition.

Sincerely,

James G. Martin
Governor

Acknowledgements

There is no way to thank everybody who contributed to the writing of *Bass Fishing in North Carolina*. But here's trying.

Ed Wood of Siler City, more than anybody else, was responsible for the success of the first edition of the book. Furthermore, this edition would not have been possible without his counsel.

The second person to whom I owe a big debt is my friend Jack Bilyeu, a former rewrite specialist and general assignment reporter for the *Washington Post*. He read the rough manuscript and caught many of my errors.

My appreciation also goes to the folks at Piedmont Impressions, the publishers of this edition. Richard Mansfield, Selby Bateman, and Tom R. Halfhill are professionals who made the work for this edition fun.

Thanks also to the people whose names appear elsewhere in the book.

In addition, I am especially grateful to William Rhodes Weaver, former "Monday Moaner" of the *Greensboro News & Record*, who kept my newspaper job going while I was out doing research for the first edition.

A number of other people contributed to the success of the first edition or this edition. They include Bob Sloan of Fontana Village, Don Knotts of Albemarle, Nat Jones of Oxford, fellow *Greensboro News & Record* staff members Stan Swofford and Jerry Bledsoe, Don Eudy of Waynesville, Bill Cloninger of Thomasville, Tom Hines of Montgomery, Alabama, and George Brumback, Ralph Bowden, Bob Gingher, Charlie Whichard, and Dave Alexander, all of Greensboro.

Also, Tom Corbett of the Appalachian State University News Bureau, Red Welch and Bob Carpenter of Franklin, Bill McCall of Highlands, Frank Dunn of Charlotte, Claude Armfield of Boone, Ray Simmons of Brevard, Richard Cole of Cherokee, Daniel Gibson of Hendersonville, Joe Steele of Lenoir, Henry Simons of Murphy, J. Aaron Prevost of Waynesville, and Bill Egerton Jr., of Weaverville.

Others who helped include Charles Heatherly, formerly of the

State Travel Section; Dick Pierce, formerly of Duke Power Company; Jim Rutherfordton of Raleigh; John Merritt, formerly of the *Fayetteville Observer*; Tom Lee and Ben Wilson of Fayetteville; and Eddie Bridges, 5th District Commissioner of the N.C. Wildlife Resources Commission.

While I was working on the first edition of this book, I met often with a group of good anglers who gather daily — every day they are not fishing — at the Irving Park Delicatessen in Greensboro. Their advice was invaluable and many of them are mentioned on other pages.

I would like to thank the others of the I.P.D. coffee drinking and fishing club: Manley Holland, "Double O." Sherrill, Jim Whitley Jr., and Jim Whitley Sr., Charlie Smith, Shortey LaRose, the Reverend Hugh Jessup, John Thompson, Morris Whitley, Henry Thompson, John Weigel Jr., Joe Hale, and C. Howell Smith.

Others who helped make the research for this book enjoyable include Cecil Martin and J.T. Warmath of Greensboro, Frank Scalia of Hartford, Connecticut, Charlie Howell of Forsyth County, Mrs. Bertha Gregory of Poplar Branch, Evelyn Meads of Elizabeth City, Kaye Woodward of Currituck County, Mr. and Mrs. Chris Parker of Belhaven, and the Hineses, O'Neals, and Baums, all of Currituck County.

Finally, the person most responsible for my having written this book is the man from whom I inherited my deep love of the outdoors, but with whom I now fish only in my memories — my dad.

Introduction

Taking A Buddy's Advice: A Fishing Book Is Born

The idea for this book was born one fall after an effortless half-day of fishing on Pungo Creek, a meandering brackish-water creek. Two nights earlier, Jack Rochelle of High Point and I had towed my skiff to eastern North Carolina. We had fished Scranton Creek the first day. Even though we caught few fish, the day was pleasant.

Jack is a congenial fishing companion, and the Indian summer day was soft, the breezes gentle. Late-blooming wildflowers dotted the marshes and the autumn foliage of the hardwood trees was in full color. There was not a hint of clouds in the cobalt-blue sky.

When we launched the skiff at dawn on the first day, there was just enough chill in the air to be invigorating. By noon, the temperature was a comfortable 72 degrees Fahrenheit. After lunch, we listened to a big buck deer thrashing in the tall marsh grass. Later, we watched as a half-dozen goldeneye duck played in the water off a bend in the creek. Every now and then, a flight of Canada geese etched a V across the heavens.

We had planned the trip by asking our friend Claibourne Darden where we should fish. Claibourne, a fine all-around sportsman, had fished the area many times. I had also called J.A. King Sr., who had fished the area for years, to ask him where we should fish. We also consulted other fishing friends, including John Peterson and former Greensboro mayor Carson Bain.

Despite all that preparation, the first day would have been fishless if Jack had not caught three bass on a shallow-running Rapala lure just as the sun was setting in a huge splash of fire. Earlier in the day, when we began to doubt we would catch anything, we joked about telephoning Claibourne and John — collect! — to ask if they had ever caught any fish in the waters they had suggested we fish. We knew, of course, that they had.

On the second day, things were to be different. Jack and I put

1

the boat in at Pungo Creek, another creek that Carson, Mr. King, John, and Claibourne agreed was a good place to fish.

About a quarter-mile from where we launched the boat, an island rose out of the creek. A colony of vultures was perched on the limbs of a dead tree on the island. The vultures' wings were spread to catch the warmth of the rising sun. Silhouetted against the sky, the buzzards looked like dark thunderbirds.

As I shut down the outboard motor, lowered the trolling motor, and prepared to fish the east shore line as Mr. King had suggested, Jack pointed out a huge hawk that was ranging over a stand of pines beyond the marsh bordering the west side of the creek. The hawk, we guessed, was looking for breakfast.

Then we saw something else. Near the edge of the creek, fish were churning the water, slashing at schools of minnows. From the way the fish were swirling, we doubted they were largemouth bass. We suspected they were either striped bass or spotted or gray seatrout, fish that often run up into the brackish-water portions of coastal-area creeks.

Despite my love of bass fishing, I was so desperate for action on this day that I was willing to fish for anything. On the hunch that the swirling fish were trout, I quickly tied a Mirrolure to the end of the line of my baitcasting rig and cast the lure into the middle of the feeding fish. The fish ignored the Mirrolure. And my fly-rod popping bug. And Jack's Rapala. And a spinner.

Finally, I again picked up my baitcasting outfit and half-heartedly flipped the Mirrolure to the marsh away from where the fish were swirling. A kingfisher that had been perched on a root jutting out into the water cocked its head at the splash of the lure, then flew away, clacking irritably at the intrusion. I began my retrieve.

The lure had moved only about two feet when something jolted it. Until I worked the fish close enough for Jack to get the landing net under it we both assumed it was a big trout. But when Jack lifted it out of the water, we saw it was a chunky largemouth bass.

At breakfast that morning, Jack and I had agreed to quit fishing at 1:30 p.m. to begin the long drive back to Greensboro. I had to be at my desk at the *Greensboro Daily News* (now the *Greensboro*

2

News & Record) the next morning.

At 1 p.m. we hefted a stringer heavy with fish. We lacked only three bass of having our limits of healthy-looking largemouth. We also had a number of big white perch and even one flounder. We caught all the fish on the side of the creek Mr. King had recommended we fish.

With the exception of the one bass that had fallen victim to the Mirrolure, the bass had all blasted fly-rod popping bugs or other topwater lures. The white perch and the flounder hit small spinners pulled slowly across the bottom.

After we had loaded the boat on its trailer and aimed my Toyota toward the west, Jack settled back in his seat and fired up his pipe.

"I'm not trying to tell you what to do," he remarked casually. "But you love bass fishing so much, why don't you write a book on bass fishing in North Carolina?"

On the trip down, I had told Jack that I was contemplating taking a leave of absence from my newspaper job. I wanted to have time to fish while I was still young enough to enjoy it. I knew I was a candidate for a heart attack. If I postponed taking some time off, it might be too late. My father had recently died of a heart attack at a relatively young age. My mother had also died young of heart disease.

Now, on the trip back from eastern North Carolina, Jack blew out a cloud of blue smoke, and added, "Instead of telling your editors you're going to take a leave of absence and just loaf, why don't you tell them you're going to write a book, and then write it?"

I don't recall my answer, but I do know it wasn't enthusiastic. During the winter that followed, however, the seed Jack had planted in my mind germinated and grew. The more I thought about it, the more appealing was his suggestion and the more sense it made.

Why not write a book about bass fishing and limit it to North Carolina? It would provide anglers with fishing facts and lore they could not find elsewhere, not even in books written by the top anglers in the country. As anyone who has fished different sections of the country knows, what fills a boat in one state can get you skunked in another state.

For this reason, there is a common weakness among even the best books on bass fishing, books written by talented national writers. By necessity, the books are too general. They are of limited use to anglers who just want to know specifically when, where, and how-to in their own home waters.

Methods that will catch largemouth and smallmouth bass often vary even from county to county within a state. In North Carolina, for example, bass in some areas will tear up a topwater bait all day long, all summer long. But in other parts of the state, if you fish a topwater bait in the middle of the day in the middle of the summer, about all you'll get is casting practice.

Why not limit the coverage of a book on bass fishing to North Carolina and explain in detail how fishing in one part of the state differs from fishing in another part of the state? This could furnish the angler with information that he could not find in any other book. Moreover, this approach should result in a more accurate picture of bass fishing in North Carolina than has sometimes been painted by writers who merely visit here, fish a day or two, then go back home and write about it. Take, for example, a story a national hunting and fishing magazine once published about North Carolina's famous Currituck Sound. The writer announced that an angler didn't need a guide to fish the sound because it was "almost impossible" to get lost.

That writer must have fished a different part of Currituck than I've ever fished. Or even heard about. It is not only possible, it is *easy* to get lost in the labyrinth of marshes, islands, ponds, creeks, and sloughs that often produce the best fishing on the sound.

One fishing friend, Roger Soles, and I were lost one late spring day for about three hours, even though we were with a guide who was a native of Currituck County. The young guide had taken us into a web of ponds where one place looked just like another to the untrained eye.

"Are you lost?" Roger asked after noticing the puzzled look on the guide's face.

The guide admitted he was. Finally, in desperation, he climbed a duck blind to get a better view of where we might be and how to get back on the open water.

The guide peered out over the tangle of marsh and water and repeated what he had just heard Roger say: "It's just a maze back in here."

As the guide poled the boat around through the ponds and interconnecting sloughs, I felt like a rat in a psychology experiment. We could see the waters of the main body of the sound over the top of the spartina grass; we just didn't know how to get out there.

To make matters even worse, I saw what appeared to be thunderheads building on the horizon. Because of a past incident at Currituck Sound, I have a great fear of lightning on the water, and I knew there was nowhere to take shelter. I became more and more angry at the guide. But then he said, "I know what I can do if I have to. I can wade out and find my granddaddy. He can tell me how to get out."

When he said that I looked at his worried face and realized he wasn't much older than my sons, then in their early teens. I couldn't remain angry at him, but I resolved never again to hire an inexperienced guide.

Roger, who was a navigator on a bomber during World War II, finally figured the way out.

It was the first and last time I was ever lost on the sound while with a guide. Over the years, I fished Currituck Sound a total of at least 60 days with my favorite fishing guide, Wallace O'Neal. He was never lost for a moment; I was lost most of the time.

Mr. O'Neal lived on Currituck Sound all his life and had been a hunting and fishing guide for more than 60 years. He probably knew Currituck better than anybody else. Yet even he had not fished all of the sound's sloughs and ponds.

I well remember one day when fishing was slow at all of Mr. O'Neal's favorite spots. He jumped up on the seat of his skiff, shaded his eyes with his hands, and scanned the marshes. Then he cranked his outboard motor and moved to a different pond.

After I had caught several nice bass in the pond, Mr. O'Neal said, "Well, you've done something new today. This is the first time I've ever been in here."

Sadly, my good friend and guide, Wallace O'Neal, died while I was writing this book. For me, Currituck Sound will never be the same.

Okay — so now Jack Rochelle's suggestion about writing a book on North Carolina bass fishing was sounding better. What next?

I called Lebby Lamb, research librarian at the Greensboro Public Library, to see if she knew if anybody had written any similar books recently. Among other places, she contacted the North Carolina State Library. Her return call clinched my decision.

"As far as I can determine, there has not been a book written on North Carolina freshwater bass fishing since the early 1900s," she said.

The fact that it had been so long since anybody had written a book about North Carolina bass fishing seemed a shame. Obviously, bass fishing had changed a lot since then. Heck, they didn't even have plastic worms in those days. Much less depth finders, oxygen meters, and electric trolling motors. Most of the man-made reservoirs we fish today weren't even twinkles in the eyes of the U.S. Army Corps of Engineers or the electric power companies.

There was another reason an up-to-date book on North Carolina bass fishing would be helpful to anglers. (Or so I began to reason.) North Carolina has some of the world's best and most varied bass fishing waters. At least one or two of our rivers, lakes, or sounds are ranked in the nation's top ten in polls conducted among famous bass anglers.

The great variety of North Carolina bass fishing waters makes the state one of the world's most fascinating places to fish. If an angler wants to cast a lure in a quiet coastal-area freshwater river where deer come to drink, North Carolina has it. If the angler wants to fish a wild and scenic brackish-water sound where an occasional eagle can be seen soaring overhead, North Carolina has that. If you live in the populous Piedmont and want to try your luck almost within sight of tall office buildings, you can find a place to do that, too. Or if you would rather fish a deep lake surrounded by majestic mountains whose tops are often obscured by clouds and where bear still roam, you can do it in North Carolina. Or if you prefer to fish for smallmouth bass in a white-water river, our state has that to offer as well.

All these things convinced me to take Jack's advice and write the book. Next, I had to decide *how* to write it.

I knew the book would have to be as specific as I could make it, even at the risk of sometimes being repetitious. Ideally, the book should cover freshwater black bass fishing from the Great Smokies to the Atlantic Ocean, area by area, river by river, sound by sound, lake by lake, and, sometimes, even creek by creek.

That created a problem. I am not an authority on bass fishing all across North Carolina. Nobody is. So how was I to get accurate and specific information that would be helpful to bass anglers?

As often happens, the subconscious provided the answer: North Carolina not only has some of the best bass waters in the world, it also has some of the top bass fishing experts in the world. Why not travel around the state and visit some of these experts? Why not ask them how they fish the waters close to their homes, waters they fish often and successfully?

That is what I did. I traveled the entire state, talking to experts. It meant lonely miles on the road, lonely nights in motels from Murphy to Manteo, and lonely meals in restaurants good and bad. But it also afforded me the opportunity to fish with and talk with people who knew more about my favorite subject — North Carolina bass fishing — than anybody else. And when my wife, Doris Dale, was able to break away and go with me, the trips were pleasant from beginning to end.

I have also recounted some of my personal fishing experiences in this book. Although I am not an expert on all kinds of bass fishing, I have fished for bass for more than half a century and have fished most of the places I describe.

Besides, as Dave Goforth, one of the state's most successful anglers, says, "You can learn something about fishing from any other fisherman — no matter how good you are and no matter how good or bad he might be."

I also reserved for myself the pleasant task of describing bass fishing in Currituck Sound and some other places in eastern North

Carolina. This is the one type of bass fishing about which I feel no modesty, false or otherwise, in discussing. I have fished these waters so many times that I feel qualified to give advice about it to anyone. Also, I love to fish the sound and other eastern North Carolina waters so much that I couldn't let anybody else have the joy of talking about it.

I make four other disclaimers:

One, this book does not include *all* the water where you can catch bass in North Carolina. It is impossible to cover all of it in one book. In some places in eastern North Carolina, you can catch bass in almost any creek.

Two, not all the water included is outstanding bass-fishing water. Although all these waters do have bass in them, some have been included primarily for other reasons: their beauty, their proximity to cities where large numbers of people live, or other redeeming characteristics.

Three, don't expect all the people in this book to be famous. It is true that a few are well-known. Yet others have never fished a tournament; have never been written about in a national magazine; and have never appeared on an outdoors program on television or radio. They all, however, have two things in common: they are great anglers and fine people.

Four, just as methods that will catch bass vary from place to place, bass fishing changes over time. Although the first edition of this book was favorably reviewed by a number of experts on fishing, one person told me years later that I had written too much about eastern North Carolina and not enough about the rest of the state. If so, there were two reasons for this: Over the years, eastern North Carolina, especially Currituck Sound, has proven itself to be one of the best places in the country to catch bass; and there is such a vast amount of bass fishing water in eastern North Carolina. It is true that, for brief periods, eastern North Carolina fishing may seem to decline and, for brief periods, other places, such as new impoundments, might seem better places to fish. But most of the new hot spots fall out of the red-hot category after the first few years.

One other thing: this book has been restricted, for the most part, to largemouth and smallmouth bass fishing. But it is impossible to discuss bass fishing without occasionally mentioning other species of fish. This is especially true of coastal-area fresh and brackish water.

Also, as Buck Perry of Hickory, one of the most learned fishermen in the country, said, "The bass is the guide fish. Once you learn to catch it, all other fish are just 'duck soup.'"

I tried in earlier drafts of the book to list the marinas where an angler can rent boats. But the next time I fished several places where boat rentals were formerly available, the places no longer rented boats. So I reluctantly deleted the list. You can write the various Chambers of Commerce or tourist bureaus for information about boat rentals in areas you plan to fish. These same agencies can give you information about places to stay.

The state publishes a directory of motels, hotels, and campgrounds. For a copy, write:

Travel Development Section
Economic Development Division
Department of Natural and Economic Resources
Raleigh, N.C. 27611

The same agency publishes a booklet about North Carolina fishing.

Wildlife in North Carolina magazine is another good source of information about North Carolina fishing. Many public libraries have back issues, and you can subscribe to the magazine by writing:

N.C. Wildlife Resources Commission
325 North Salisbury Street
Raleigh, N.C. 27611

My friends and I have also found an old publication called *A Catalog of Inland Fishing Waters of North Carolina* to be a valuable tool in our fishing. The publication is now out of print, as far as I can determine. But some public libraries have copies. It has detailed information on every stream in the state, including their location, size, and the species of fish they contain. It also has information on where you can launch your boat.

The volume is based on a U.S. government study done many years ago, and much of the information is out of date. Still, it is the most complete guide to North Carolina freshwater and brackish-water fishing areas that I have ever seen.

By the way, about five years after I wrote the first edition of this book, I suffered the heart attack I feared I might have some day. I had it, ironically, after a successful day of fishing on Currituck Sound. I recovered, and I hope to catch many more fish before my ashes are scattered over Currituck Sound or some other North Carolina sound, river, lake, or creek.

Enough about the background of this book and general information on North Carolina bass fishing. Let's go cast a lure or maybe even dunk a minnow.

Part 1:

Eastern North Carolina

Quiet, Uncrowded Fishing

Chapter 1

Fishing Like It Used To Be

Claibourne Darden and I were fishing one spring day in a creek that runs into the Pungo River in the Belhaven area of Beaufort County, not far from the North Carolina coast.

We were moving along slowly and silently under power of the boat's electric motor when Claibourne turned and whispered, "Look at that fawn over there."

I strained my eyes until I finally saw the fawn. She was lying in the marsh grass right at the water's edge and appeared to be just enjoying the scenery. With her white spots and big, appealing brown eyes, the fawn looked like Walt Disney's Bambi.

Claibourne quietly reached for his camera as I edged the boat closer to the marsh. The fawn let us come very close. But when the camera clicked, she stood up and bounded off.

Later, on the way back to the motel, we saw two grown deer standing beside the road.

Those are the kinds of things that make fishing trips to eastern North Carolina so soul-satisfying, even on the rare days when you don't catch fish. Much of the water is still unspoiled. You can fish some stretches for miles and not see a thing to suggest that any person has ever been there before you — not even a beer can or a candy wrapper.

Much of the good bass water in eastern North Carolina has been neglected because many natives would rather catch saltwater fish. Despite the neglect (or because of it), the largemouth bass fishing is sometimes sensational.

You can use a powerful bass boat on many of the creeks,

13

rivers, lakes, and sounds of eastern North Carolina. But some of the water is so shallow and weedy that a low-cost aluminum boat or an old-fashioned, homemade wooden skiff will do better — just as long as it is stable.

For the most part, such new-fangled gadgets as depth finders and temperature meters are unnecessary. Fishing here is much like it was in the good old days.

Roger Soles, who later became chief executive officer of Jefferson-Pilot Corporation, introduced me to this kind of fishing in the mid-1960s. He invited me on one of his Currituck Sound parties. I enjoyed it so much that I started going back several times a year on my own. For years, I fished Currituck an average of four times, or eight days, a year. The fishing was so good that there were few times when I did not catch my limit of bass.

While not as famous as Currituck, practically all of the fresh and brackish water of eastern North Carolina offers some good largemouth bass fishing. True, coastal-area streams are not celebrated for big bass. Yet they do give up a number of lunkers each year. The Chowan River in northeastern North Carolina is one of the best places in the state for big bass, and I have seen a number of bass over eight pounds that came out of other coastal-area waters.

One was caught by Kemp Reece Sr. Kemp and his son, Kemp Jr., once accompanied my younger son, Conrad, and me on a trip to Currituck. It was the first time that either Kemp Sr. or Kemp Jr. had ever fished for bass. Kemp Sr. was using a spincasting reel and a Pflueger Chum spoon. On one of his first casts, he hooked and landed a bass that weighed more than eight pounds.

Jimmy Hines, Kemp's guide, described what happened: "I was watching his spoon in the clear water, and I could see the bass about to hit the spoon. I told him, 'There's a bass straddling that spoon.'"

What did Kemp do?

"I just rared back and started winding," Kemp said later.

On the same trip, Kemp Jr. hooked a bass that Jimmy Hines judged to be even larger than the eight-pounder. You can guess what happened. Just as Kemp Jr. got the fish almost to Jimmy's landing net, the fish swirled. The line popped.

Kemp Jr. was only about nine years old at the time.

"I looked at him right after that happened," Jimmy said. "His mouth curled up and big tears filled his eyes."

Kemp Jr. had no reason to be embarrassed; losing a bass of that size would bring tears to the eyes of an adult.

Joe Kyle, another Greensboro friend, boated a Currituck bass that weighed better than eight pounds while I was fishing with him. Joe caught the bass on a gold-plated Johnson weedless spoon. Sometimes, a big bass can be sluggish for its size. That wasn't true of Joe's bass. Even though Joe hooked the bass in heavy underwater weeds, the bass shot out of the water like a rocket. Then it headed away from the boat in a run I thought was going to wrench the reel from Joe's hands.

Finally, as the bass appeared about to give up, it made a lunge under the boat. That maneuver bent Joe's rod until the tip was about two feet under water. If Joe hadn't had the equanimity to loosen the drag, he not only would have lost a fish, he would have needed a new rod.

One of the most fascinating true fish stories I've ever heard is about a 7.5-pound bass that got away from another friend, Paul Schenck. How does he know it weighed exactly that much? He knows all right. He has both a witness and pictures to prove it.

The bass walloped a Johnson silver spoon, and Paul skillfully led the fish to his guide's landing net. The guide scooped the fish up and weighed it. Paul made a picture of the guide holding it. The guide made a picture of Paul holding it.

The guide put the fish on a stringer. Then the guide threw the fish in the water. The fish promptly swam away with the stringer. The guide had forgotten to tie the stringer to the boat!

"I really felt sorry for him," Paul said of the guide. "He spent his whole lunch hour poling around, looking for the bass."

Johnson spoons seem to be a favorite of big Currituck bass. That's what Tom Fee, another fishing friend, was using on one of his first trips to Currituck Sound when he caught a bass that weighed better than eight pounds.

Somebody forgot to tell Bob Ingram, still another friend, that bass don't grow very big in eastern North Carolina. In one morning of fishing on Currituck, Bob caught nine bass that weighed a total of 25 pounds. He caught one eight-pounder and one five-pounder on consecutive casts. And he caught them all in one spot.

The largest bass I ever heard of being caught on Currituck weighed more than 12 pounds. It was caught, believe it or not, on a fly rod. But the fly rod was in the hands of the late Joe Brooks, the great fishing writer and one of the best fly-rod anglers of all times.

Other eastern North Carolina waters give up an occasional big bass. A bass hanging on the wall of a Gates County ABC (state liquor) store weighed better than 11 pounds. It was caught by Charlie Mullen, a clerk in the store. He caught the giant in Merchants Mill Pond.

Howard Carr has caught a number of large bass in eastern North Carolina. His largest came close to nine pounds. He caught it in Tranters Creek, a tributary to the Tar River near Washington, N.C.

Hunter Galloway, a Greensboro automobile dealer, caught a bass in eastern North Carolina that weighed almost nine pounds.

Still, a big bass is the exception in eastern North Carolina — much more of an exception than in the Piedmont and western parts of the state. For that reason, most people who fish the eastern part of the state don't expect to catch many large bass. They do expect to catch more fish than they would normally catch in most other parts of North Carolina, or almost anywhere else in the United States.

Most of the time, even a beginner should have little trouble catching at least some bass in North Carolina's coastal-area fresh and brackish waters.

Eastern North Carolina largemouth bass waters range from small, sheltered streams you can fish in a modest-sized boat in a near gale, to vast open rivers and sounds that can be turbulent and dangerous in a high wind. Even streams that are called "creeks" can be as wide as a mile in some spots.

Although some of the water is so free of weeds that you can fish almost any type of lure without getting hung up, much of it is so weed-infested that you can fish it only with topwater or weedless lures. On some of the water, you fish under canopies of moss-laden cypress trees. But on other water, there is nothing but low-lying marsh as far as you can see.

For the most part, the water is shallow, and depths of more than six feet are rare. But a few spots are deep. I once recorded a depth of better than 40 feet on a narrow stretch of the Pungo River. Some stretches of the Tar River and some of its tributaries are very deep, too, as are some parts of the Roanoke River and its tributaries.

Of all the conditions affecting bass fishing in coastal-area fresh and brackish water, wind is the most important. The wind blows the water either into the streams or out, depending on the direction of the wind and the location of the stream. That creates what natives call a "wind touyide." Most often, a northeast wind will blow the water out. Then fishing is exceedingly difficult. The lunar tide has no measurable influence on most of the coastal-area largemouth bass fishing, despite the area's close proximity to the ocean.

One of many things that makes a fishing trip to eastern North Carolina pleasant is the residents. Stopping for a break or a meal at Hertford, Edenton, Belhaven, and other communities is like visiting a storybook town.

The people still have time to be friendly. They live at a more relaxed pace than people in the large cities. When you walk down the streets in one of the small eastern North Carolina towns, almost everybody smiles and speaks. At a cafe or at a soda fountain in a drugstore, people pass the time of day with you in a neighborly fashion, and they will go to great lengths to help even a stranger. Just like the fishing, eastern North Carolinians are much as they used to be.

I will always remember the day Bill Keys and I burned out a wheel bearing on my boat trailer right outside Conway, N.C. Somebody told us that the best place to get it repaired was at Murfreesboro. But by the time we got to the center of Conway, the wheel was wobbling so violently and making such a racket we knew the axle was going to break any minute.

We pulled into the first garage we saw. There we met a retired gentleman who introduced himself as Clarence "Clem" Taylor. He explained that the garage was owned by his son-in-law.

"I'm just here passing the time of day," Mr. Taylor said. He added that he knew something about boat trailer wheel bearings because he liked to fish himself. "But I don't go in too much for freshwater fishing. I do saltwater fishing mostly."

He would be glad, he said, to see what he could do to help. He removed the wheel and took out the bearings so he could get the model number. The bearings were so chewed up they looked more like sand than metal.

Mr. Taylor suggested we go to a farm equipment company that would probably have a set of bearings to fit my trailer.

"Let's go in my car," he suggested. "That way, you won't have to unhook yours from the trailer."

At the farm equipment company, we found the correct bearings and returned to the garage, where Mr. Taylor installed them and packed them with grease. Just to be sure everything else was in working order, he removed the bearings from the other side of the trailer and repacked them with grease, too.

The operation took about two hours of hard, dirty work. But when I asked Mr. Taylor how much we owed him, he replied, "Oh, how about a dollar and a half?"

Bill and I tried to get him to take at least $10. But he refused it and walked away. We caught up with him and stuffed $5 into his shirt pocket. I had never seen Mr. Taylor before, and I will probably never see him again. But I will never forget his kindness.

I will long remember similar incidents.

One day while seven friends and I were fishing in four skiffs on Currituck Sound, a nor'easter suddenly blew up. The sound became so rough that I wondered if we would survive. But back at the fishing lodge that night, a count showed that the worst thing we got from the experience was a scare and some spray-soaked clothes.

At dinner, as we were discussing the harrowing day, the telephone rang.

"That was Booty," Mrs. Bertha Gregory, the lady of the house, explained after she had hung up the telephone.

She was referring to Booty Spruill, one of the best-known

guides on Currituck Sound. He had called to see if we'd all survived the blow. It had been, he said, the roughest day he'd ever
experienced on the sound. What made the call so thoughtful was
that Booty wasn't even one of our guides.

I remember still another pleasant encounter with another
eastern North Carolinian, William T. Smithwick. Three friends and
I had pulled our boats up to the landing at Mr. Smithwick's campground for lunch. As we prepared to cook under a picnic shelter,
Mr. Smithwick walked down to greet us. He took one look at the
few bass we had caught that morning and decided we didn't have
enough to eat. He insisted I go with him to his freezer, where he
loaded me down with fresh flounder fillets. Not only did we have
flounder for lunch, but there was plenty left over to bring back
home.

Another time, my car got stuck at a boat landing as Wilt
Browning and I were launching my boat at Scranton Creek.

"I think we're going to have to get a tow truck to pull us out,"
Wilt said after the wheels of the car dug deeper and deeper into the
soft earth.

Leaving Wilt to watch the car and boat, I got out on the highway and stuck out my thumb. A pickup truck, the first vehicle that
came along, stopped. The driver, who introduced himself as Ross
P. Lane of Spring Hope, had been saltwater fishing.

He gave me a ride to Belhaven. There, a service station opera-
tor told us that the only place in town that had a tow truck was an
automobile dealership, Cox Chevrolet. Ross Lane then drove me
there and stayed until he was sure I could get help. He refused to
accept money for his trouble.

"I hope you have some luck fishing," he said as he drove off.

The owner of automobile dealership, who introduced himself
as Jimmy Cox, said sure, I could get me a tow. "I hope you don't
mind waiting a minute," he said. "The man who drives the tow
truck has started undercoating a car, and when you start that, you
need to finish it without stopping."

Jimmy came out of his office and sat and talked to me while I
waited, which was not very long. I asked Jimmy if I could go ahead
and pay. "I'd like not to have to come back," I explained. "I want

to go fishing."

Jimmy said that would be fine. Although Scranton Creek is about 20 miles from Belhaven, the cost of towing our car was only about $25. When I expressed amazement about how little it was, Jimmy said, "We still believe in doing things the small-town way."

That kind of friendliness is characteristic of the people of eastern North Carolina. If you are fishing an area for the first time, don't hesitate to ask residents for advice. They will be glad to share their secrets with you. You may have to search for awhile, however, to find anybody who knows anything about bass fishing. Most of the locals are more interested in saltwater fishing.

When I first started fishing the coastal area for bass, I found a publication called the *Coastal Fishing & Vacation Guide* to be helpful. It has maps showing where various species of fish, including largemouth bass, can be caught. As far as I can determine, the guide is no longer published. But some libraries still have old copies.

Another thing you should buy is a navigation map of the area you plan to fish. You can buy these at many marinas, yacht basins, and tackle stores along the coast. Or you can order them directly from the government. A free catalog that describes the maps can be ordered from:

U.S. Department of Commerce
National Oceanic and Atmospheric Administration
Distribution Division, C-44
Riverdale, Maryland 20840

This is one government agency that is prompt. The maps also are economical. But there may come a time when you would not sell one for a thousand dollars. In addition to telling you where you are, the navigation maps will give you a good idea of water depths. That, of course, is valuable information to an angler.

A compass is also a good investment for fishing this water, where one place often looks like another.

Topwater,
All Year
— Almost

Chapter 2

Southeastern North Carolina

According to the calendar, the month was February, and it was cold on the Trent River near New Bern in southeastern North Carolina. Dale Reed Flickinger used the electric motor on his bass boat to ease into a cove. Then he lowered his thermometer into the water.

The river was ten degrees warmer than the other water he had fished that day.

"I couldn't believe my thermometer," he recalled later.

But just for the heck of it, he changed to a topwater lure. On his second cast, the water bulged and the lure disappeared. Dale Reed set the hook and cranked in a small bass.

He chuckled as he later recounted the incident. "I must have caught about 15 in the 2-pound bracket, all on top. None of them was big, but they all were good fighting fish."

Admittedly, that doesn't happen very often in the winter, not even in southeastern North Carolina. But it does illustrate one reason why that area holds such a special charm for many bass anglers. Winters are warmer and topwater fishing begins earlier in the year and lasts longer than anywhere else in the state. And what angler doesn't get a special thrill when a bass explodes through the water's surface to engulf a floating lure?

The unique fishing of the brackish and freshwater streams of southeastern North Carolina made Dale Reed Flickinger, a Californian, forsake his native state and become a Tarheel. He also became one of southeastern North Carolina's most knowledgeable bass fishermen.

I met Dale Reed through Hugh Rich of Jacksonville, North

21

Carolina. Although Hugh, a successful insurance man, didn't fish, he admired the dedication and skill that goes into excellence — whether it be in fishing or insurance.

The first time I met Dale Reed, I talked to him in the den of Hugh's attractive home overlooking a particularly beautiful stretch of the New River. Dale Reed first became acquainted with the local bass fishing when he was in the U.S. Marines and stationed at nearby Camp Lejeune.

"I had fished out on the West Coast since I was a tot," he said. "When I first started fishing here, I couldn't believe there were so many bass and so few bass fishermen."

The fishing around Jacksonville was so fantastic that Dale Reed remained in North Carolina after retiring from the Marines.

He smiled again. "I told my wife, 'You'll never get me out of this country.'"

Dale Reed bought a fully equipped bass boat and started fishing at least four or five times a week around his home in Maysville. "I decided to live in Maysville because that is in the middle of the fishing grounds," he explained, as a smile flickered across his sun-bronzed face.

He ticked off his favorite fishing waters:

— The Cape Fear and Northeast Cape Fear Rivers in the Wilmington area, and their many tributaries.

— Southwest Creek, the White Oak River, and the New River and their tributaries, all in the Jacksonville area.

— The Neuse and the Trent Rivers and their tributaries in the New Bern area.

— The Tar River and the Pamlico River and their tributaries, especially Tranters Creek in the little Washington area.

"All the creeks and rivers around here have freshwater bass in them," Dale Reed declared.

They also have something else in common: They are affected much more by the wind than are the rivers and lakes farther inland.

"A strong wind either blows the water in or out, depending on the direction of the river or creek," Dale Reed explained.

Most often, a strong northeast wind will blow water out of the rivers and creeks and toward the ocean. A strong southwest wind, on the other hand, will usually blow the water back in. The water level can change several feet in a few hours. In the shallow water of these creeks and rivers, that's a lot.

The fishing is almost always better when there is plenty of water.

"That's especially true in the spring and summer when the weeds are coming up," Dale Reed said. "Then all you have to do is work topwater lures over the weeds."

In some of the water, weeds are so thick you have difficulty fishing even with weedless lures. Goose Creek on the Neuse River, one my favorite fishing spots, is typical. It has plenty of bass, but plenty of weeds.

You can catch fish with any type of gear in southeastern North Carolina. When I looked in Dale Reed's boat, however, I saw that he had both spinning and bait-casting outfits. He said a person should have at least one fast-retrieve rig for working buzz baits and spoons that have to be skittered across the top of the water.

Dale Reed said he used a fly rod occasionally, especially on the White Oak River. "It's good on that river. You know, that's a funny river. Bass don't get big, but there are a lot of them, and they fight like the devil."

A few months after I met Dale Reed, I fished the White Oak River for the first time. Harry Gianaris and I fished in my boat. Two of our friends, Bill Black and John Peterson, fished in John's boat. As often happens even in the best fishing places, the fish did not cooperate. But I caught enough bass on my fly rod to confirm what Dale Reed said: They fought like the devil.

As we fished the White Oak, a strong tide washed in. The river is one of the few freshwater bass streams that has a lunar tide. Dale Reed speculated that the tide is one reason why coastal-area bass have more spunk than bass that live elsewhere. "My theory is that they fight so hard for their size because they are always having to fight the tide or the current or something else," he remarked. "They are constantly fighting for survival."

If you're going to fish these waters and you own a fly rod, you should take it along. A fly rod and a topwater bass bug can be both deadly and exciting on any of the waters of southeastern North Carolina. One reason the fly rod is so good is that the water is, for the most part, shallow. Consequently, bass will blast a popping bug for up to eight months a year.

"We start using topwater baits right now," Dale Reed said. It was early April.

Surface lures remain effective through the spring and summer and right on through November, if the weather doesn't get unusually cold. Sometimes, as Dale Reed found out on that February morning, largemouth bass will greedily hit topwater lures on days when people in the Piedmont and mountain sections of the state are worrying about whether snow will fly before nightfall.

Dale Reed said he had two favorite topwater lures. "The Devils Horse is about the best around this neck of the woods, especially in areas where you don't have a lot of surface weeds or lily pads," he said. "Then when you get to weeds and lily pads, you should go to the Weed Wing."

The Devils Horse is, of course, a floating wood lure that has small propellers, usually on both the front and rear. It is best fished with a twitch of the rod to make the propellers spin and give off a gurgling or rattling sound. It apparently imitates a wounded minnow. When there is a big chop on the water, the lure should be fished with vigor to make more noise.

Unlike the Devils Horse, the Weed Wing doesn't float naturally. It is a weedless metal spoon that has to be fished fast to make it skitter across the top of the water. That's why an angler should take along at least one fast-retrieve outfit. The Weed Wing has a large propeller on the front that whirls when the lure is raced over the water's surface. The manufacturer recommends that the lure be fished with a pork frog.

"The Weed Wing makes a sputtering racket, like a minnow breaking the surface or something like that," Dale Reed observed. "It comes in numerous colors and sizes."

The quarter-ounce gold Weed Wing is especially effective on southeastern North Carolina coastal-area streams. But bass, being fickle, sometimes prefer other sizes and colors.

Dale Reed said he switched to sub-surface offerings when bass
ignored his topwater lures during spring, fall, and summer. His
favorite sub-surface lures include Bomber Speed Shads and shallow-running Rebels. They also make good cold-weather lures.

"Those are the best danged producers I have found in the
winter," Dale Reed declared. "When the water gets real chilly, say
around 42 to 43 degrees, the bass just tear up the Rebels and Speed
Shads."

One January, Dale Reed caught his limit four days in a row on
the Trent River. His lure: a Bomber Speed Shad. The lure runs only
about four feet deep.

He said he seldom caught fish more than three or four feet deep
— even in the winter. "I know that goes against all theory that the
bass should be deep in January. But there's almost always deep
water close to where I catch bass in shallow water in the winter."

The spinner bait is another favorite winter lure among southeastern North Carolina anglers. Dale Reed said his favorite colors
in lures were yellow and raccoon perch (yellow interspersed with
dark circles).

What did he think of plastic worms?

"If I had to choose one lure for all seasons," he answered
without hesitating, "it would be the plastic worm."

The plastic worm should be fished in southeastern North
Carolina about like it is fished in other places. Most anglers fish the
worm with a "Texas rig." This, of course, involves pushing the
hook through the worm, then turning the worm around and imbed-
ding the hook into the worm to make it semi-weedless.

A slip sinker is generally used above the worm. The worm
should be fished with the lightest slip sinker that's practical for the
depth you are fishing. When the wind is blowing hard, of course,
you have to use a heavier weight.

In southeastern North Carolina, the worm is usually fished in
shallow water, no matter what time of year. Most anglers cast their
worms to the same targets they cast to when using other types of
lures.

"Most of the time, we hit the cypress knees and kind of drop it
down as we're coming into shallow water from deeper water,"

Dale Reed said. "We get some real good fish that way."

In areas where there are no cypress knees, southeastern North Carolina anglers cast to obstructions such as brush, stumps, tree tops, and other objects that stick out of the water.

Dale Reed said he occasionally bumped the worm across the bottom in deep water, but not very often.

Asked how fast he retrieved the plastic worm, he said, "I bring it in real slow, stopping it occasionally and taking up the slack in the line. Some people will use the worm in the spring basically like they use it the rest of the year. But I like to use it lots of times without a sinker, almost like a topwater bait. I use the Mr. Twister worm or others that have tails that wiggle on the retrieve. I reel it in fast, and the tail gurgles across the weeds and lily pads, and the bass just knock it silly."

He listed his favorite colors in plastic worms as purple or blue in solid colors, or blues with fire tails. The "motor oil" worm — one the color of fresh motor oil — has also become popular with coastal-area bass anglers in recent years.

People fishing southeastern North Carolina for the first time have many spots from which to choose. Bass fishing can be good in any of the rivers. Dale Reed, however, hesitated when asked to name his favorite stream. He said he was glad he wasn't restricted to just one stream.

Finally, he answered. "The Trent River. The Trent River has got a lot of 18- and 19-foot holes. It's got grass. It's got lily pads. It's got pilings. It's got the works for bass. That's the one I would choose."

And his favorite time of year?

"The spring," he said. "I like the spring even better than the fall."

He agreed that an angler's chance of catching a big bass in southeastern North Carolina is not as good as it is in the inland reservoirs. "But we do catch some big fish," he said. "In our bass club we have an average of 20 members, and I'd say we catch at least a hundred bass a year that weigh over five pounds [each] in the waters around here."

Dale Reed estimated that club members will land, during a

typical year, a total of three or four bass that weigh from 8 to 10 pounds. The Trent River gave up one bass that weighed 10.5 pounds, Dale Reed said. That's another reason why the Trent is his favorite river. "But we do not catch a lot of really big lunkers," he admitted. "Over seven pounds is an exceptionally big fish."

The fighting instincts and the numbers of bass in southeastern North Carolina make up for their lack of size. The brackish and freshwater streams of the coastal area support phenomenal numbers of largemouth bass. And the bass are often easy to find and easy to catch.

Dale Reed thinks one reason there are so many bass in coastal-area streams is that they have a wider variety of food than do their inland cousins. "They have bait fish, crawfish, fiddler crabs, all kinds of menhaden, and many other things to eat," he observed.

While most of the water described by Dale Reed is shallow, there are some deep spots. For that reason, many anglers who fish the area use depth finders. "There is one spot on the Trent River that ranges from 48 to 52 feet. But the average is probably no more than 8 feet."

To fish southeastern North Carolina, you don't need all the modern gadgets of a fancy bass boat. The main requirement is that your boat be capable of handling rough water. The coastal area is subject to squalls and storms. And they often come with little warning.

You can fish the sheltered creeks of the southeast in a small boat, however. A friend, Joe Kyle, and I once fished Goose Creek off the Neuse River in a 12-foot, shallow johnboat. We had no trouble — even though we could see whitecaps out in the river.

You should always carry a compass, though. Heavy fogs can roll in quickly. When that happens, you have difficulty seeing the end of your boat, much less the sun. At those times, it's impossible to feel your way across even a moderate-size creek without a compass. If you watch what you're doing, use a map, and carefully choose your landmarks, you should be able to fish most of the water without getting lost.

You do need to bring some kind of boat with you to fish most of southeastern North Carolina. "I don't know why, but there are few places where you can rent a boat on these rivers," Dale Reed said. He added that members of the Bass Anglers Sportsman Society (B.A.S.S.) can often find a fishing companion who owns a boat by contacting one of the B.A.S.S. clubs in the area. This, of course, should be done well in advance of your trip.

One of the pleasant things about fishing coastal-area streams for largemouth bass is that most of the streams are still uncrowded. Many natives are more interested in the good saltwater fishing that is nearby. Also, most of the largemouth rivers and streams are not particularly suitable for water skiing, so there's less of that than there is farther inland. "Even on the weekends, it's not very crowded," Dale Reed noted.

There are many good motels and hotels in the area. Wilmington, Jacksonville, and New Bern are all within easy reach of good bass fishing. You might want to bring your family and stay at one of the beaches in the area. The good will you gain will more than make up for the extra distance you have to drive to reach the bass fishing water.

Other Southeastern Waters

_____ Chapter 3

Black River, White Lake, And Others

If you enjoy the solitude and scenic beauty of bass fishing almost as much as you enjoy catching bass, at least once in your life you should fish one of the remote, cypress-lined, black-water rivers of southeastern North Carolina.

The Black, the South, and the Waccamaw are three of the prettiest of these rivers. All are known more for their redbreast sunfish than for their bass. But they can give up some very good bass, too.

Even if you don't catch a bass, a day on one of these streams will renew your soul. Long stretches of the water look untouched by man. Big cypress trees, with their beards of moss, lend the rivers an eerie beauty. Dignified, stilt-legged white herons wade the shallows so slowly that they seem motionless. But then their rapier bills will dart into the water with strobe-like quickness to spear a minnow. And as you round a bend in one of the rivers, you sometimes see a big buck deer plunge into the water and swim to the other side.

If you are real lucky, you might even spot a bear. And there are still some sturgeon — the prehistoric fish from which caviar comes — in these rivers. In the lower reaches, migratory saltwater fish move into the rivers during some seasons of the year.

There are ospreys, wild duck, kingfishers, and even an occasional eagle. There are a few houses and cabins along the shores, but most have been designed to blend in with their natural surroundings.

One of the most enjoyable (though least productive) fishing

trips I've ever taken was on the Black River. Ben Cone Sr., who owned property and a vacation lodge on the river, invited Claibourne Darden to use the lodge for a weekend. He told Claibourne to bring some friends. Claibourne asked John Ellison, John Peterson, and I to go with him. Mr. Cone was not able to go with us, but he instructed the overseer of the property, Dennis Hollaman, to guide us and help us any way he could.

Dennis, a personable man and an authority on the wildlife of the area, added much to the enjoyment of the trip. He fished with us and joined us for meals at the Cone lodge. He said he didn't specialize in bass fishing. He asked Jerry Barnes of Atkinson, a good bass fisherman, to tell us something about the bass fishing in the area.

Jerry, a native of the region, fished the Black River on many evenings after work and on weekends. He fished the year-round. "The bass fishing is not as good here as some other places," he conceded.

Yet he had caught a number of nice bass from the river himself, and other members of his bass club had also done well. "I saw one bass that weighed 12 pounds and 6 ounces that came out of the river," Jerry said.

His choices of times to fish the Black River? April and May. His advice on lures? Simple: spinner baits and plastic worms all year long. "I use the same tactics in the winter that I use in the summer. I just slow the baits down a little in the winter."

He made his own spinner baits and preferred blue or yellow. He said that he enjoyed fishing topwater lures when conditions were right. Those are good on the Black, Waccamaw, and South rivers all day long during the spring and fall, and in the early morning and late afternoon in the summer.

The only other lures Jerry mentioned were the shallow-running thin-minnow type lures, such as the Rebel and Rapala. These are especially good on the Black and other nearby rivers in the spring.

Don Shealy of Fayetteville, one of the state's best shallow-water fishermen, disagrees with the popularly held opinion that the Black River is not a good stream for bass. No wonder — some of the bass he's caught in the river look as if they came from Florida, a state known for its huge bass.

"The bass are just harder to find on the Black River," he said.

Don told about how he once discovered a concentration of nice bass on the river.

"I found a bank down near Wilmington that had about six or seven little tributaries coming into it," he said. "The first day I found it, I caught 30-some bass in there in about a 200-yard area. The tide was coming out. The fish in that area feed basically on crawfish and fiddler crabs. That bank was just literally stacked with fiddler crabs and crawfish — and bass."

Don returned to the area two days later.

"I carried a friend of mine, Terry Williams, a good fisherman, and we fished most of the morning, and we had only about four fish. When we got down to that same bank, I told him I knew where some fish were, and I told him, 'Terry, I want you to tie on a spinner bait. It doesn't make any difference what color.' Then I said, 'I'm going to put you on a place here, and I don't want you to tell anybody about it,' and he said, 'All right.' So he and I went over to that same bank and we caught, I think, about 30 bass."

Don said he also liked to fish the Cape Fear River close to his Fayetteville home. He used about the same methods to fish the Cape Fear, Black, and Waccamaw rivers that he used on other shallow-water streams. (See Chapter 5 for a description of these methods.)

If you want to fish the Black River downstream, which is the prettiest part of the river, the Atkinson area is a good place to put your boat in. There are several good launching areas near Atkinson, including two operated by the North Carolina Wildlife Resources Commission. People in the Atkinson area are friendly, and you can get directions to the landings at almost any service station, general store, or other business.

When water levels are near normal, you can use a motorboat with little difficulty on most of the river around Atkinson. But there are a few places where you may have to pick your way carefully around sandbars, fallen trees, and sunken logs. Some places on the Black River become impassable at low water, or when there has been enough wind or high water to uproot trees and block the river.

There is always something interesting to see on the Black River and similar rivers. On the weekend we fished the Black River, we were fascinated by the small one-person boats used by residents of the area. The boats are so tiny that they appear unsafe. Some people use small paddles that look like Ping-Pong paddles. Holding a paddle in each hand, they deftly move their little boats so fast that you'd think they were using a small outboard motor. Dennis Hollaman told me that this method of powering a boat dates back to the Indians, who introduced it to the white settlers.

Some anglers actually do rig these small boats with electric motors. The motors are the hand-controlled type, but the ingenious Black River anglers rig them with blocks of wood and strings so they can guide the motors with their feet. Presto! They have a foot-controlled motor for the price of a hand-controlled motor.

You'd think it would be nearly impossible to lose your way on rivers such as the Black River, the South, or the Waccamaw, but you can. It is often difficult to find a distinct landmark. Many stretches with their majestic cypress trees look just like other stretches. Although the main bodies of the rivers are generally narrow, creeks feed into the rivers, and there are many large coves on the main waterways.

When you go back into one of the tributaries or coves, fish for an hour or two, and then re-enter the rivers, you sometimes forget which direction is the way home. Dennis suggested a way to determine which way you're traveling. You simply shut down your motor and let your boat drift. Or you watch the leaves and twigs that have fallen into the water to see which way they are drifting. That tells you which way the current is moving and whether you're headed upstream or downstream.

There are a number of other rivers or lakes to fish in southeastern North Carolina, including White Lake and Lake Waccamaw. These lakes are not particularly known for their bass fishing, but they do have some bass.

You have a wide choice of places to stay when you fish any of this water, including Fayetteville, Wilmington, Clinton, Lumberton

(where you could also fish the Lumber River), and many smaller
towns in between. You can even rent a cottage at White Lake or at
one of the other Bladen Lakes.

The Pasquotank River

Chapter 4

Also, Little River And Big Flatty Creek

A light dusting of frost lay on the ground in Greensboro when the sun came up that mid-October morning. But by the time we arrived at Elizabeth City, more than 200 miles to the east, the air was milder.

Still, when I thrust my hand into the Pasquotank River's dark water, the river seemed cool. So *Greensboro News & Record* columnist Jerry Bledsoe and I went out into the river and fished artificial worms and other underwater lures to try and catch a bass. We didn't get a strike for several hours.

"Let's do something new," I told Jerry. I cranked the engine on my small skiff and headed to Sawyers Creek.

I had crossed Sawyers Creek, one of the prettiest streams I have ever seen, many times in my automobile. Each time, I thought how much I'd like to fish it. A friend said he once stopped at the creek on the way back from the Outer Banks and caught a lot of big bluegills. Jerry and I changed our bass lures for small spinners and tried fishing for bream. Even they ignored us.

Frustrated by our lack of success, we returned to the canal leading to the boat-launching ramp. There we met our friends Woody Tilley and Van King, who were fishing in Woody's boat. They had caught several bass on topwater lures without even going out into the river. Jerry and I quickly replaced our underwater lures with Jitterbugs and caught several bass.

If I had remembered what Dr. Regis Dandar had told me several years earlier, we wouldn't have waited so long to switch to surface lures.

"I've caught them up to December on top," he had said.

On the same morning he told me that, he said he'd once had a modest aim. "My goal was to catch a five-pound bass," he declared.

Before you scoff, you should know the background of that statement.

Regis's first experience with North Carolina bass fishing was at Fort Bragg, where he served as an officer in the U.S. Army. Before coming to Fort Bragg, he had fished for bass only in Pennsylvania, where he was born and raised. If you don't already know it, a five-pound bass is considered a lunker in many states north of the Mason-Dixon line. That includes Pennsylvania. So it was natural for Regis to begin sampling the North Carolina bass fishing, trying to catch that five-pounder, while he was stationed at Fort Bragg.

As it turned out, something else happened.

"The first bass of any size that I caught was not five pounds," Regis, a dentist, recalled. "It was eight pounds."

That eight-pound bass helped change Regis's life. Instead of returning to Pennsylvania to practice dentistry when he got out of the army, Regis decided to hang out his shingle in Elizabeth City in North Carolina. "Bass fishing had a lot to do with my coming here to the South to live."

As soon as he moved to Elizabeth City, he began fishing as often as his dental practice would allow. He fell in love with nearby Pasquotank River, a stream that has everything from narrow stretches that meander through cypress forests to wide-open reaches where seatrout sometimes mingle with largemouth bass. When I first met Regis, he modestly denied that he was an expert on Pasquotank River fishing. He said he hadn't lived in the area long enough (at that time he had lived there about five years). Nevertheless, he had applied a combination of common sense and scientific deduction to his bass fishing, and it is doubtful that many other people knew more about the subject of bass fishing on the Pasquotank than he did.

The Pasquotank is in northeastern North Carolina. It contains bass throughout much of its length, including the stretch that passes right through Elizabeth City. The river suddenly opens up just outside the city and becomes ever wider until it empties into Albemarle Sound.

"The Pasquotank is not particularly noted for its bass fishing," Regis said. "But there are a lot of bass in the river."

By now you may be tired of hearing this, but the reason the Pasquotank is not particularly noted for its bass is simple: As in other coastal areas, many people who live near the Pasquotank are so interested in saltwater fishing that they overlook the often sensational freshwater bass fishing.

"Part of the problem of fishing the Pasquotank for bass is that there are not enough bass fishermen that you can get information from," Regis said. "The fishermen who probably catch most of the largemouth bass in the Pasquotank are from Virginia."

As soon as he became a resident, Regis began fishing the Pasquotank the year-round. "But I do better in the spring and fall," he said. "Those are the classic times."

What advice did he have about lures for that time of the year?

"We do well with rubber worms," he answered. "The rubber worm is very versatile. You can fish it in shallow water. Or you can fish it right down to 30 feet with an adequate sinker."

He said he also liked topwater lures in both the spring and the fall. And in the summer, too. "We've got plenty of structure on our shorelines where a bigmouth can find a little shade, even in the summer," he explained. "There is always a potential for fishing the shoreline with a topwater bait."

Regis said he usually started off with topwater lures in the spring and fall. If they failed, he switched to artificial worms and spinner baits, working them around stumps and submerged cover. "A lot of the boys from Virginia prefer the bigger spinner baits. In fact, I've caught some nice bass on the spinner bait. The bass have a tendency to like the fiery-red colors, the new fluorescent colors."

Apparently the fluorescent colors are more visible to the bass in the Pasquotank's cypress-stained water than most other colors. "In topwater fishing, the blues seem to be good," Regis said.

The favorite topwater lures on the Pasquotank include shallow-running Rapala and Rebels or other thin minnow-type baits. They are usually fished by twitching or popping them on the surface. If the bass ignore the lures on top, they can be retrieved so they work just under the surface.

"Sometimes, we do real well with the broken-back or jointed Rebel or Rapala," Regis said. "At other times, the bass won't hit anything but the one-piece Rebel or Rapala."

Regis also recommended the Devils Horse for topwater fishing on the Pasquotank. Sometimes, Pasquotank bass will snub everything but a topwater lure even in the middle of a hot summer day. "I've had a frustrating morning, not catching anything," he said. "Then, just as I was getting ready to give up right around high noon, I've spotted some breaking activity and caught fish on top. For some reason, they occasionally feed well right around noon in the hot summer."

Regis advised casting to breaking fish even if you know the fish aren't bass. At times, there will be one or more big bass under the school, even if the school is composed of gar or other unglamorous fish.

Despite an occasional success with topwater lures in the middle of hot summer days, many anglers normally use plastic worms at those times. "I try to get the plastic worm in among the cypress trees and other shaded areas and work it real slow," Regis said.

Translucent worms in strawberry and other reds show up well in the dark water of the Pasquotank. "Along towards evening purple can be good. And I take a couple of blues and blacks along just in case."

Other popular worms on the Pasquotank include the Mr. Twister, Creme Flip Tail, and others with curly tails.

"We have some deep cuts in some parts of the river where the water drops to ten feet real fast," Regis said. "I have a lot of confidence in that type area, and a lot of fishing is just having confidence. I chuck the worm out on the bank and let it work both the deep and shallow-water areas. I try to keep it on the bottom."

In this kind of area, the quarter-ounce slip sinker is usually the best size to use. In real shallow water, the eighth-ounce or even lighter slip sinker is better. Regis said he switches from his bait-casting rod to a spinning rod when using worms with sinkers lighter than eight ounces.

Many anglers think fall is the best time for topwater fishing on the Pasquotank. Regis agreed. "I start really getting enthusiastic on topwater, and I have more confidence the bigger bass will be hiding around the stumps in the fall."

Just as on other parts of the North Carolina coast, topwater fishing on the Pasquotank starts earlier in the year and lasts longer than it does in inland North Carolina.

The fly rod can also be deadly on the Pasquotank, especially in the spring and fall, and during early mornings and late afternoons in the summer. Medium-size popping bugs in black and various shades of blue and yellow are usually good.

Regis said he began using the artificial worm more as the water cooled and then, with the approach of winter, switched to spinner baits and lures, such as the Little George.

Anglers who fish the Pasquotank during the winter look forward to February and March. "I think your biggest bass are going to be caught towards the end of February and into March," Regis said. "They start looking for places to bed even as early as that. It seems the theory is that the bigger bass move on the beds first. The big ones will be on the shoreline then. That's about the only time of the year you can guarantee they are going to be in four or five feet of water. It's often cold then, but they do start looking for places to bed. You might find them off the points and use a spinner bait or a worm. March is the month of the lunker."

There is some water skiing on the Pasquotank, but it doesn't create a problem for the bass angler. Most of the good bass fishing is in areas unsuited for water skiing. A person can often fish all day long on the Pasquotank and not be disturbed -- not even by other bass anglers.

Regis had been introduced to me by an old friend, Don Whitley, then general manager of the *Elizabeth City Advance*. Don was a good newspaperman and a fine man in general. He was no slouch as a bass fisherman, either.

Don lived right on the Pasquotank. He kept a boat ready to go at all times. When he got the urge to go bass fishing, all he had to do was step out of his house, walk a short distance, and jump in his boat.

"The real ironic thing about Pasquotank bass fishing is that people who live here just don't get into it," he said. But he added that the lack of bass fishing on the river had nothing to with the quality of the bass fishing.

Don fished the plastic worm almost exclusively. Like Regis, he prefers February and March for big bass. "And I mean they're really aggressive then," Don declared.

Both Don and Regis said that small boats are suitable for fishing the upstream portions of the Pasquotank. "But below town, she can really blow, and you might have some problems," Regis warned.

"The river gets pretty wide [below town] for small craft," Don added. "You have some places where it gets to be about three miles wide."

The moon tide has little effect on the Pasquotank. But the wind can cause some fluctuation in the water levels, depending on which direction the wind is coming from. A strong northeast wind usually lowers the water level.

"We call that a 'wind tide,'" Don said.

But unlike Currituck Sound, where a strong northeast wind blows out so much water that is almost impossible to fish, there is almost always enough water on the Pasquotank for fishing. Currituck is only about 18 miles to the east of the Pasquotank.

"I don't know that the water level makes too much of a difference on the Pasquotank," Regis said. "It's the changing of the water level that seems to influence the fishing more than the actual depth."

Although the northeast wind generally hurts the fishing in most of the coastal-area fresh and brackish water, the bass often go on a feeding spree during the early stages of a northeast wind. The Pasquotank is no exception. It's almost as if the bass know that they had better gorge while they can, that many of their favorite dining areas will soon be high and dry.

Elizabeth City has several good motels and restaurants. If you like a good barbecue or seafood dinner after you fish all day, you can find some of the state's best in this town.

There is a municipal boat ramp near the downtown section of Elizabeth City. There are also a number of other places to launch a boat on the river, including a ramp operated by the North Carolina Wildlife Resources Commission.

The Little River and Big Flatty Creek — despite its name, Big Flatty is more of a river than a creek — are both within easy driving distance of Elizabeth City. Both offer good bass fishing and can be fished using the same methods that are good on the Pasquotank.

The Chowan River

Chapter 5

Want To Catch A Big Bass?

How would you like to catch a ten-pound largemouth bass?

If your answer is yes — what other answer is possible? — Don Shealy has some advice.

"If I had to go to one single place in North Carolina to catch a ten-pound bass," he told me, "it would be the Chowan River."

We were sitting in the air-conditioned den of Don's Fayetteville home. We were surrounded by mounted trophies of deer, other game animals, and, of course, by several huge, mounted bass. There were also many plaques and certificates attesting to Don's skill as a sportsman. Don will be remembered for many years as one of the nation's best shallow-water anglers.

When I first talked to Don about fishing, he didn't have time to fish in as many bass tournaments as some of the "professional" anglers. He was too busy working as the full-time manager of a Lowe's hardware store. Yet he had already compiled a remarkable record in the tournaments he had entered. He had won two national tournaments — including the first one he ever entered. The other national tournament he had won was a fly-rod tournament, an accomplishment that showed him to be a particularly skilled and versatile angler.

In addition to the nationals, he had also placed first in a dozen or so other major tournaments. He had lost count of the local and regional tournaments he had won, there had been so many. A pretty good record for a man who was basically a weekend angler.

The Chowan River, Don's first choice as a place to fish for big bass, is formed by several Virginia rivers. It flows through north-

43

eastern North Carolina and enters the Albemarle Sound near the historic and quaintly beautiful Edenton, a town that dates from early colonial days.

The best fishing on the Chowan probably starts northwest of Winton in North Carolina. The fishing, however, is excellent throughout the river's length.

Don, speaking of the Chowan, recalled, "I fished one tournament up there — it was a boat tournament — that was won by two boys who had 14 fish that weighed a total of 56 pounds. That's an average of four pounds each!"

Even more remarkable, Don added, was the fact that the average for each boat in the tournament was 30 pounds of bass.

On the same day as that tournament, one angler brought in a largemouth bass that weighed 12 pounds 7 ounces. "He was not even fishing in the tournament," Don said. "He was just fishing."

Although there are some fairly deep holes in the Chowan, it is, for the most part, a shallow-water river. Don said he fished the river using much the same methods he used in other shallow water. Don fished the Chowan year-round, but he said he preferred to fish March and April during a normal year.

What are the best lures for those months?

"I would use a worm or spinner bait that time of the year," Don said. "An eight-inch blue worm seems to be the best as far as catching real big fish."

Despite that, however, Don said he usually tied a spinner bait on his line first. He had a good reason for that. "If fish are hitting at all, the spinner bait is the fastest way in the world to catch your limit. If they are not hitting it, it won't take you but 20 minutes to find out."

In tournament fishing, Don usually switched to artificial worms after catching his limit on a spinner bait. His theory was that while he would often catch more bass on a spinner bait than on a worm, he would probably catch bigger fish on the worm. After switching to the worm, he began "culling" his fish, replacing the smaller fish he caught on spinner baits with the larger fish he caught on worms.

One reason Don likes the Chowan is the type of cover and structure characteristic of the river. Among other things, the

Chowan has what Don called *inside* and *outside* cypress trees. *Inside trees* are those that grow near the shoreline. The *outside trees* are those that stand in deeper water, farther out from the shoreline. If the fish are hitting shallow, the inside trees are good places to fish. If the fish are hitting in deeper water, the outside trees are the best places to fish.

Don said he fished the spinner bait in a variety of ways around the cypress trees. "I might throw it beyond a tree and buzz it up to the tree. Then the next time, I might try coming up there and let it fall and then yo-yo it up and down. You've got to try different things."

Don said that later in the spring, he liked to start off the day with a topwater bait and then, as the sun climbed higher in the sky, switch back to the spinner bait or worm. He returned to the topwater lure late in the afternoon.

That's another reason the Chowan is so much fun to fish. "It's a real good place to fish topwater due to the type of things you've got on it," Don said. "You've got the big cypress trees, and you've got other types of structure. It's just a perfect place for topwater."

Don listed his favorite topwater baits: the Devils Horse, the South Bend Nip-I-Diddee, and the Heddon's Tiny Torpedo. He said he also liked the Bang-O-Lure, a thin-minnow lure that can be fished either on top or slightly below the surface of the water. The Rapala and the Rebel, of course, operate on the same principle as the Bang-O-Lure, and are also good on the Chowan.

I prefer the plastic thin-minnow lures such as the Rebel rather than the Rapala or other balsa-wood lures. The plastic ones are a little heavier and easier to cast in a breeze. Some anglers think the balsa lures catch more fish because they are more life-like. But I just about always catch fish on a plastic thin-minnow lure when my partner is catching fish on a balsa thin-minnow.

Topwater lures should be fished tantalizingly slow on the Chowan when possible. If the water is rough, you should give the lures more action.

Don said he used about the same tactics during the summer that he used in the spring. But he recommended that an angler try diving baits in hot weather, along with the worms, spinner baits, and topwater lures.

Don said he continued the same basic tactics in the fall, but used topwater lures for longer periods during the day than in the summer.

He said he fished spinner baits almost exclusively in the winter. Then, however, the baits should be worked slower, because the bass are usually a little more sluggish than they are when the water is warmer.

Warner Perry was a young man who had fished the Chowan River most of his life when I called and asked if I might stop by to chat. Like most people who live in eastern North Carolina, he was hospitable. "Sure," he said. Come on by."

He agreed with almost everything that Don Shealy said.

"There are some big bass in there," he commented matter-of-factly. "There really are."

Warner grew up in Colerain on the banks of the Chowan, but lived in Edenton when I visited him. He expected to live out his life in eastern North Carolina. "I'm about as far west as I ever want to get," he said.

Like Don, Warner believed the best time to fish the Chowan is March, before the herring spawn, and into early April. March, he said, is the prime month. "Of course," Warner said, "there is some cold, blustery weather then, but that's when bass fishing is best and I think it peaks out after that."

Still, Warner made it clear that even if the bass fishing "peaks out" about April, it remains excellent all year long when compared with most other places.

What are the best lures to use in March?

"I'd use plugs, the River Runt, broken-back Rebel, or some-thing similar," Warner said. "Or I might try a worm. And the spinner bait can be mighty good."

Like Don, he pointed out that deep diving lures can be used on the Chowan without difficulty. "There are not a lot of weeds on the Chowan. You have a lot of stumps and cypress knees and that sort of thing."

There are some weeds in a few spots, along with some lily pads. But especially in March and April, they present little problem because they're not usually up yet. "There is practically no milfoil or anything like that," he said, referring to the Eurasian aquatic grass that has grown over much of Currituck Sound. When the milfoil is in full growth, it is difficult to use anything but a weedless lure on the sound.

What lures would Warner use on the Chowan as the water gets warmer in the spring?

"I might go to some topwater stuff on into May," he said.

What kind of topwater stuff?

"Well, the Jitterbugs is a mighty good bait. The Hula Popper or something of that nature can be good. Or a popping bug on a fly rod."

Warner said he liked to use those around the cypress knees. He agreed with Don that topwater lures can often produce good results through the summer, especially early in the morning or late in the afternoon.

Warner liked the artificial worm during the summer. He remembered the first time he ever used them. "A friend and I tried them out. We had never heard of them before then. It was hot as blazes, and we didn't even know how to use the worm. But we went out and fished some of the deep water stumps, and we caught seven or eight bass the first day we used them. We had bass that weighed five and six pounds. The plastic worm is a mighty good bait."

Warner said he also liked to use a diving plug in the summer, one that will bang the bottom. The Chowan does have some deep holes, even though most of it is shallow.

"If you're fishing the stumpy areas near the shore, you're probably not going to find much water deeper than seven or eight feet," he said. "But there are a lot of deep water stumps, old trees, and whatnot that are considerably off-shore, maybe a half-mile. And off some of the points, you find water that is 12 or 14 feet deep."

He said he most often fished the worm with a heavy weight, as much as a half-ounce, to take the worm down deep.

Warner said the River Runt Spook is the all-time favorite lure on the Chowan, especially among residents of the Colerain area. "There has a been many a bass caught on that lure," he said. "It's a mighty popular bait over there."

Warner confessed that the winter was not his favorite time to fish. "Usually, when it gets real cold, I'm out trying to chase a duck or something of that nature." But still, he said, the winter can be a good time to catch bass on the Chowan.

The Chowan is now more famous for bass than it was when Warner was growing up. "We see a lot of the B.A.S.S. club members coming in now," he said. "Right here in Queen Anne's Creek, we see three or four boats practically every weekend in March."

Queen Anne's Creek is a tributary to Edenton Bay and Albemarle Sound near the mouth of the Chowan. The creek is just a short distance from where Warner lived when I visited him.

Despite the increasing popularity of the Chowan among bass anglers, the river is so big that it's not usually crowded. And the vastness of the river, which is several miles wide in some places, offers another advantage: It is almost always possible to find protection from the wind — you simply make a run to the side of the river that's calm. Much of the river is sheltered along the shore by large trees. There are also some creeks running into it that offer protection.

Warner said the Colerain area was his favorite place to fish the river. There is a boat launching ramp in Colerain. "About two miles north of Colerain, there is some beautiful water," he said.

Don Shealy said his favorite place to fish was in the Tunis area in Hertford County, especially around Holiday Island. There is an N.C. Wildlife Resources Commission boat access area at Tunis. There are also two Wildlife Resources boat access areas in Chowan County and one in Gates County. Privately operated landings are scattered throughout the length of the river.

Ahoskie and Edenton are convenient places to stay, depending on the part of the Chowan you decide to fish. In addition, Murfreesboro is within a reasonable distance of the Chowan and offers the interesting possibility of fishing both the Meherrin River and the Chowan River on the same trip. There is a Wildlife Resources Commission boat access area on the Meherrin near Murfreesboro. The Meherrin, a tributary to the Chowan, offers the same general type of bass fishing as the Chowan.

Other rivers in the area that offer excellent bass fishing are the Perquimans and the Yeopim. There are places to launch a boat on both rivers, including a Wildlife Resources Commission access area on the Perquimans. The Perquimans, especially near Hertford, is also known for better than average-size bass. A good place to stay and to launch a boat is at Hertford, which has a municipal ramp.

The Chowan, like most other coastal plain streams, seldom gets too muddy to fish. It has had some pollution problems. At one time, there was even speculation among experts that it could become a "dead river." But thanks to crackdowns by federal and state authorities, the situation has apparently improved.

At any rate, many knowledgeable anglers — in addition to Don Shealy and Warner Perry — have long rated the river as one of the best largemouth bass habitats in the state.

Merchants Mill Pond, near the Chowan, is another interesting place to fish. The pond is on Bennetts Creek, a tributary to the Chowan. The pond is only a little over a thousand acres in size, but it has lots of bass, and some big ones. There is a fine specimen of a Merchants Mill Pond bass on the wall of the Gates County ABC store on Highway 158 near Gatesville. I heard about the bass and stopped at the store to see it — and to talk to Charlie Mullen, who caught it. (What else other than a big bass would tempt me to enter an ABC store?)

The bass, when Mr. Mullen caught it, weighed 11 pounds 7 ounces. "I caught it on a Beetle," Mr. Mullen said. "Actually, it was a crappie-size lure." He was fishing the small lure without a spinner behind the spillway when the monster bass grabbed it.

Although Mr. Mullen caught that big bass on a crappie lure, the artificial worm is the most popular lure among anglers who regularly fish Merchants Mill Pond. (The pond contains a lot of obstructions.) Other than that, you can fish the pond just about as you would fish any other water in northeastern North Carolina: topwater in the spring, and in the mornings and late afternoons in the summer; Rebels or Rapalas and other shallow-running lures, along with weedless spoon, from spring to fall; spinner baits, especially in the cold weather; and about any other lure you can fish around debris.

Merchants Mill Pond is in Gates County. Normally, the pond is not crowded.

By the way, Don Shealy said he believed that good spincasting gear was the best all-around tackle for water where there are many low overhanging limbs. Don said he seldom used baitcasting gear. When Don pulled out his spincasting gear in the first national tournament he fished, his partner laughed at him. But by the end of the day, his partner had quit laughing.

"As soon as I get home," the partner said, "I'm going to buy me one."

Don said he liked spincasting gear because it is so easy to use. "You can fish it side-armed, overhanded, or underhanded," he noted.

The Alligator River

Chapter 6

...And Others Close By

The first time I fished the Alligator River, I didn't own a boat. I borrowed my dad's, and Curtis Youngblood and I towed it all the way from Rock Hill, South Carolina, across North Carolina to Columbia, N.C. We arrived in time to have dinner at the motel restaurant with our friends Claibourne Darden and John Peterson.

The month was early April, but March had not gone out like a lamb. The weather was blustery. We barely managed to catch enough fish the first day for Claibourne to cook lunch on the river bank. The next day, however, the waves sloshed ashore with so much force we knew we'd have difficulty putting our boats in the water. Reluctantly, we decided to give up and return to Greensboro.

On the way back to the motel, we passed some men walking along the swamp that adjoined the highway. The men were carrying metal rods. "See that?" I asked Curtis. "Those men are hunting for snakes."

"Ha, ha," Curtis said. "I'm not going to fall for that."

I had pulled so many practical jokes on Curtis that he no longer believed anything I said. But after we checked out of our motel and stopped at a service station for gasoline, we saw the men. Several wire cages rested in the rear of their station wagon, which bore Pennsylvania license plates. The cages held snakes and other reptiles.

The men said they were from Philadelphia and that they hunted snakes as a hobby. They said they took the snakes home and gave them to zoos, natural science museums, or other educational institutions. By coincidence, the men worked for Pennsylvania Bell

51

Telephone Company. Curtis worked for a sister company, Southern Bell, in Greensboro. The Philadelphians said they took a week's vacation each year to travel to eastern North Carolina and hunt for snakes.

I asked one man what his wife thought about him spending a week hunting snakes.

"What the hell does *your* wife think of you taking time off to come down here to fish?" he said.

I didn't have an answer for that.

The Philadelphia snake hunters said they came to the Alligator River area to hunt snakes because the area is in a *climatological transition zone*. In other words, the climate, they said, has some of the characteristics of a subtropical region and some of the characteristics of a northern region. Therefore, the area has some snakes that are native to the northern climates, and others — such as the coral snake — that are native to tropical climes.

If you think about it, that's also why eastern North Carolina waters hold such a wide variety of fish. On that trip, before the wind became too violent for us, we caught jack, crappie, white perch, and yellow perch, along with a few bass. This wide variety of fish also means that largemouth bass in the Alligator River area have many types of food to eat, and it helps explain why bass fishing on the river is so good.

Despite the good fishing, the river is usually uncrowded. On some days, your only company will be ducks, deer, herons, Canada geese, and other wild creatures. One reason for the light fishing is that the river is relatively inaccessible. Then, too, the Alligator's reputation is overshadowed by the more famous Currituck Sound, only a short distance away. Yet the largemouth bass fishing on the Alligator can be fabulous, especially if you go armed with a little knowledge of the area and have enough good luck to catch the right weather conditions.

"I think that it's the finest [bass] fishing place in the world," Dr. J. Baxter Caldwell once told me.

He knew what he was talking about. He had owned a second home near the Alligator River for more than 20 years and used it to escape the pressures of his dental practice for a day, a weekend, or a week, as often as possible. Baxter had been fishing the Alligator even longer than he had owned a home there. He had fished the river and its tributaries regularly since the end of World War II.

Asked to name is favorite method of fishing the Alligator, Baxter replied, "I use a fly rod 90 percent of the time. I guess I'm kind of a funny fisherman. I just like to catch them on top."

Maybe more of us should try to be funny about our fishing -- Baxter caught a lot of fish. He fished all over the northeastern part of the state, from Currituck to Collington and from Collington to the Alligator. "But most of my fishing has been in East Lake, South Lake, and the Alligator River," he said.

East Lake and South Lake are all part of the same body of water. They join together and feed into the Alligator River, which cuts through parts of Dare, Tyrrell, and Hyde counties. If you travel the area on U.S. 64, you cross the north end of the river between Manns Harbor and Columbia.

Baxter said his favorite bass fishing spot was Second Creek, a tributary to the Alligator River. "Second Creek is about four miles south of the Alligator River Bridge," he explained. "You can put your boat in right there at the Shell service station. They've got a landing. Then you just run right down the shore about four miles."

Another of his favorite places to fish was the Little Alligator River, which flows into the Alligator River near Albemarle Sound. "The Little Alligator is about a half-mile north of the bridge," Baxter explained. "It runs back west."

He also liked South Lake and East Lake, north of the bridge and on the east side of the river. "Fourteen years ago, if I had to go one place in the world to fish for bass, it would have been South Lake," he declared. "I would catch more and bigger fish. You hardly ever caught anything under two pounds."

South Lake is still a good place for bass, but is not nearly as good as it once was. Humans have changed it for the worse. Among other things, canals have been dredged around the lake. "It is a lot darker now and has a lot more acid in it," Baxter said.

There is an N.C. Wildlife Resources Commission boat launching ramp on East Lake. By launching there, you can fish both East and South lakes without making the long run up the Alligator River to reach them. The Alligator in this area is open to the elements and can get rough in a blow. This is especially true when the wind howls out of Albemarle Sound into the mouth of the river.

Baxter said he also enjoyed fishing the Frying Pan area of the Alligator River south of Second Creek.

Another reach known for its good bass fishing is the Gum Neck area south of Columbia. The N.C. Wildlife Resources Commission has a launching ramp there, too. Most of the river, in fact, is accessible from boat launching ramps. In addition to the ramp at the bridge and the two operated by the Wildlife Resources Commission, there are several others. Some of the ramps are well maintained, but others are unimproved and not adequate for large bass boats. If you want to explore the river, you would do well to seek the advice of local residents about where to, as many of them say, "put your boat over."

Baxter Caldwell sounded almost apologetic when he confessed to sometimes putting his fly rod down in favor of a spinning or baitcasting rod while fishing the Alligator. "That's usually when my arm gets tired and I can't use a fly rod," he explained.

Even when using a spinning or casting rod, Baxter said, he tried to stay with topwater offerings. His favorites: Jitterbugs, Tiny Torpedoes, and others he described as "old standbys."

He also mentioned the shallow-running Rebel. "That's been pretty good to me. You can play it on top or underneath." Rapalas, Bang-O-Lures, and other similarly shaped lures are also good.

Baxter said he preferred topwater lures in spring, summer, and fall. He confessed to occasionally using underwater lures when he could not entice a bass to the surface. When that happened, he said, his first reaction was usually to try the Johnson weedless spoon with pork rind. "Plastic worms, and your spinners — such as the Mepps — are also big," he said.

There are a lot of cypress trees, willows, and marsh grass on the Alligator, along with some milfoil. However, on many sections of the river, it is clear enough to permit the use of non-weedless lures.

The wind has some effect on water levels of the Alligator and its tributaries, but not as much as it does on some other eastern

North Carolina waters. Still, it can put a damper on the fishing. "When the wind comes out of the northeast and it gets up to, say, 20 miles an hour, you might as well go home," Baxter declared. "The fish just won't bite."

The Alligator is primarily a freshwater river. "It's slightly brackish, but not as brackish as, say, Currituck or Collington, because it is farther from the ocean," Baxter explained. "When the wind blows out of the north or the west very much, you can't even taste the salt. If it blows out of the south, however, the water will get a little brackish."

Most people who regularly fish the Alligator agree that on most days in warm seasons, the fly rod is an excellent way to catch bass. When bass are hitting well on top, however, they will blast any surface lure, in addition to the fly-rod popping bug.

Baxter said his favorite color in popping bugs was yellow. He also liked whites with a little red mixed in. "Black can also be good. I've caught the three biggest bass I ever caught on a fly rod on black and white poppers I make. But on most days, yellow will be the most productive."

In plastic worms, the colors that catch fish in the rest of the state will do well on the Alligator. These include the black, purples, and blues, along with motor oil and other translucent colors. In Rapalas and similar lures, the colors that imitate bait fish are good. The silvers and golds are best. Apparently, the silver and gold lures remind the bass of small white perch, yellow perch, or other silver or yellow minnows.

In metal spoons, the silvers are usually the best. But at times, the golds do better. Occasionally, when bass are following a spoon all the way to the boat without striking, a knowledgeable angler will switch to a black spoon. This happens most often when the sun is bright and the water is clearer than normal — clearer than a dry martini. Some anglers who don't have black spoons darken their silver or gold spoons by burning them with matches.

Although Alligator River bass fishing is among the state's best, you won't catch many lunkers on the river. A six-pounder is unusual. There's no doubt there are larger fish in the river, but they're just not caught very often by sports anglers.

Baxter Caldwell recalled a day when he and a fishing friend saw some commercial fishermen at work at the mouth of East and South lakes. "We pulled up to see what they had caught," Baxter said. "They had some largemouth bass in their nets, which we didn't get a chance to weigh because they were throwing them back in. [It is illegal to keep largemouth bass that are caught in commercial nets.] But some would have gone 12 or 14 pounds."

Baxter said he felt spring was the best season to fish the Alligator River, and that fall ranked a close second. Few people fish the Alligator for largemouth bass in the winter.

Depth finders are less necessary on the Alligator than on deeper inland waters because most of the river is too shallow. "I have one in my boat," Baxter said, "but I hardly ever turn it on."

You don't have to worry much about water skiers running you off the water on the Alligator, or about some hot dog speeding down the river so fast that he has to wear his cap backwards to keep it from blowing off. There are too many stumps and logs in the Alligator for fast boating. "You can fish sometimes all day long, and you won't even see another boat," Baxter said. "That's what I like about it."

Eating and lodging accommodations in the vicinity of the Alligator River are limited. You'll find a few places at Columbia and Manns Harbor. There are, however, many motels and restaurants in the beach communities of Manteo and Nags Head, just a short drive away.

Another tributary to the Albemarle Sound, the Roanoke River, offers fishing similar to that of the Alligator River. The Roanoke runs into Albemarle Sound at the sound's extreme southwestern end, near the mouth of the Chowan River. I've caught at least a few bass every time I have fished the Roanoke.

Phelps Lake is also a good bass fishing lake. But two other lakes in the area, Pungo Lake and New Lake, are not generally considered great lakes for bass fishing.

As the Philadelphians said, there are many kinds of snakes in eastern North Carolina, including some that are poisonous. When I fish that part of the state, I often see cottonmouth water moccasins

that look as big around as my arm and as long as I am tall. I've never heard of one getting into a boat. Still, I carry a snakebite kit in my tackle box.

Currituck Sound

Best Bass Fishing In The U.S.?

I felt like the little boy who gives his father an electric train for Father's Day because the boy wants a train set. My conscience bothered me. Then the bass swirled at Dad's Hula Popper.

It was Dad's first cast. He didn't expect the strike and failed to set the hook. The bass spat out the lure, turned, flashed a big white belly in the clear water, and swam away.

I had brought Dad to Currituck Sound for a Father's Day present. The reason my conscience was hurting was that I chose the trip to Currituck partly because I wanted to go myself. Currituck Sound is my favorite place in the world to fish. But I felt much better when the bass hit the Hula Popper. I knew from the big smile that spread across Dad's face when the bass struck that I had chosen the perfect Father's Day gift, even if it was also a little selfish on my part.

When the fish got away, our guide, Wallace O'Neal, scolded Dad. "You shouldn't have lost that fish," he declared. "It's bad luck to lose the first one!"

Mr. O'Neal was seldom wrong about anything that had to do with Currituck Sound bass fishing. On this day, however, he was to be proven wrong about our impending bad luck. By noon, we had 15 bass on the stringer.

I caught mine on a fly rod and a popping bug. Dad caught his on a spincasting outfit. Although we weren't intentionally competing, neither one of us could get very far ahead of the other. Every time Dad caught a fish, I would catch one just a few minutes later.

A light rain fell sporadically. It was a nice rain, just enough to keep the June day comfortable.

When noon arrived, my stomach growled. I suggested to Mr.

O'Neal that we stop fishing long enough to eat. He refused. "Fish a little while longer and get your limits," he said. "The next time I have a fishing party, I want to be able to tell them, 'The other day, I had two fellows down here who caught their limits before lunch.'"

We needed only one more fish to reach our legal limit, which at that time was eight bass each. As often happens, however, the fish suddenly stopped hitting. We fished for about another hour without a tap. Mr. O'Neal finally pulled the boat up to the marsh, and we broke open our lunch boxes.

Dad finished his lunch first. He picked up his rod and cast his topwater lure about 30 feet beyond the boat. The lure landed in an open spot in the aquatic grass. Dad twitched it slightly. *Splash!* A medium-size bass was on it.

Dad talked for years about how much fun he had on the trip. Although he had fished for bass every few days in South Carolina, where he lived, this was his first trip to Currituck. He agreed that the fishing on the sound was as good, or better than, he had heard it was.

Currituck Sound, in the extreme northeastern corner of North Carolina, may well be the best largemouth bass fishing spot in the world. It is true that the bass you catch usually will not be as large as bass further inland. But day in and day out, during most years, you will catch more fish on Currituck than at any other place I have ever fished, including Florida. And you will catch enough lunkers to keep you hoping that, on the next cast, you will get one large enough to qualify as a decoration for your den wall.

Currituck is an immense and unspoiled sound that covers almost 100,000 acres. Its average width is four miles. It is so vast that on some days you can't tell where the sky ends and the water begins.

The sound is also hauntingly beautiful. On its eastern side, it is separated from the Atlantic Ocean by a long sliver of land — a string of barrier islands, the Outer Banks. It is one of the few places in the world where you can catch largemouth bass — a strictly freshwater fish — while listening to the roar of the ocean. The sun bathes the sand dunes that loom over the Outer Banks in a soft pink light, making them appear much closer than they really are.

Currituck's marshlands, not yet tamed by man, support a wide variety of wildlife. Ospreys soar overhead. If you're real lucky, you might even see a bald eagle. Marsh hares as big as Texas jackrabbits peer out of the grass at you. Raccoons don't stop their fishing as your boat passes by. In the fall, the air is filled with the sound of honking Canada geese, and ducks wait until you are almost upon them before taking off.

I love Currituck Sound and its people so much that I've told Doris Dale and my sons that I want my ashes scattered over the sound someday, or that I be buried in the little cemetery on Church's Island. The cemetery overlooks the sound and is the final resting place of my old friend and fishing guide, Wallace O'Neal.

Bynum Hines, a Greensboro friend, once captured my feelings about Currituck in a few words. It happened after the guides for our fishing party of six people met at noon at an abandoned shack on the eastern marsh so we could enjoy one of Claibourne Darden's delicious shore lunches of fresh bass, hush puppies, and other trimmings.

Connie Bennett and I fished together that morning. When Johnny Owens, our guide, pulled his skiff up to the shack, Claibourne already had his portable stove fired up. Paul Schenck was helping him cook. Reed DeVane was cleaning fish. Connie got out his knife to help Reed clean fish.

Bynum was off to himself, making slaw, one of his specialties. When I asked him if I could help, he handed me a head of cabbage and a grater. As we sat shredding the cabbage, I commented on how beautiful that stretch of the sound was. Bynum agreed. "If a man looks at that and still doesn't believe there's a God, he's in trouble," he said.

When I attended Bynum's funeral a few years later, the memory of what he had said that pleasant spring day made it a little easier for me to accept his death.

Currituck Sound is brackish. The rivers that flow into it from Virginia are freshwater streams, but they are lethargic and don't have the energy to push out all of the salinity that intrudes from the Atlantic Ocean. For that reason, you sometimes taste salt when you put your fly line in your mouth to help control it after you hook a bass. In fact, there is enough salt in Currituck to support some fine flounder fishing. I remember when two anglers in our fishing party of eight — Bill Black and Hargrove "Skipper" Bowles — caught a washtub full of flounder on Currituck after catching their limits of freshwater bass in the morning.

From time to time during its evolution, Currituck Sound has contained enough ocean water to be classified as a salt-water, rather than brackish-water, sound. Ocean water poured into the sound through inlets. Each time, one of the storms that frequently sweeps across this stretch of the "Graveyard of the Atlantic" closed the inlet. The last time this happened was in 1828 when a hurricane closed New Currituck Inlet. Sometimes you still catch bass over oyster shell beds left from the years when the sound had as much salt as the Atlantic Ocean. Now, the only salt that reaches Currituck seeps through Oregon Inlet on Albemarle Sound, many miles to the south, or from the ocean, even farther south.

Yes, I love Currituck Sound. Yet like some beautiful women, the sound is fickle. One hour it can be warm and soft. The next hour, almost without warning, it can change to a thing that is cruel. Gales are common and, over much of the sound, there is nothing but low-lying marsh to protect you.

Two New York friends, Jose Martin and Marvin Klapper, once got a taste of Currituck's violent side. Jose, a well-known big-game angler, was no stranger to rough water. Neither was Marvin, textile editor of *Women's Wear Daily*, who often fished Long Island Sound in his own boat.

It was a fine day when Jose and Marvin landed at the Norfolk Airport. They rented a car and drove down to the hunting and fishing lodge to meet the other six of us, who were from various parts of North Carolina. The fishing was good, though not sensational, at least not by Currituck standards.

When the guides brought their boats to the dock of the hunting and fishing lodge to pick us up the next morning, the sun was just peeping over the eastern marsh about five miles across the sound, and its rays coruscated deep red on the water. The moisture on the spider webs sparkled brightly, making the marsh look as if it were covered with diamonds. It promised to be a perfect day.

One of our guides casually mentioned that the forecast called for strong northeast winds. That was hard to believe; there was only a ripple on the water.

I had drawn Joe Kyle, a Greensboro friend, as a partner. After our guide, Eddie Wheatley, made the two-mile run across the sound and stopped his skiff on a point for us to fish, there was still only a slight breeze, and it was coming from the south.

I don't believe I've ever seen bass hit any better than they did that morning — for about 30 minutes. We got strikes on almost every cast. The fish weren't choosy about what they smashed: my fly-rod popping bug or the Tiny Torpedo that Joe was using on an open-face spinning outfit.

Soon, however, we began to lose more fish than we caught. Then I realized what had happened: The wind had picked up, causing our lines to curve, no matter how hard we tried to keep them tight. This made it difficult to set our hooks.

My arm soon began to throb from the effort of driving the fly-rod bug into the wind. That wasn't unusual for Currituck, where you almost always fish in some wind; a dead calm is as rare as a nine-pound bass. The sky was still a diaphanous blue, the shade it was to remain for the rest of the day. But the wind had now drifted around and was coming from the east.

Then it happened. The wind moved a few degrees toward the north, turned into a nor'easter, and roared down the sound, driving sheets of spray across the water. Eddie Wheatley gritted his teeth and leaned his whole body into his push pole, straining to keep the boat in a position for us to make decent casts.

Reluctantly, I suggested to Eddie that he pull the boat up to the marsh so we could have a cup of coffee and see if the wind would blow itself out. It didn't, and we decided to quit fishing and return to the hunting and fishing lodge.

Although the sky continued clear, we were forced to wear rain suits to keep from getting soaked by spray as we crossed the turbulent sound. We had to shout to be heard above the howling wind. I thought we were going to swamp.

Back at the lodge, we met Jose and Marvin. They had also decided to call it a day. Jose's face was still ashen. "We had a harrowing experience," he declared.

Jim Donovan of Charlotte, who was on his first trip to Currituck, put it another way: "It was rough. Whoeee!"

We had all been afraid that we were going to end up in the water that day. That's what had happened to two of our anglers, Jim Boyles and Duncan Stephenson, on another Currituck trip. The wind simply turned their boat over, though they survived the experience with nothing worse than some wet clothes and a few lost lures. (Ironically, Duncan was killed in an automobile accident a few months later.)

The fact that Currituck gets rough is only one reason why you should hire a guide, unless you own a stable boat and are thoroughly familiar with the sound. You will also stand a better chance of catching fish if you employ a guide.

On many days, you should have little trouble catching fish. When conditions are anywhere near ideal, Currituck fishing is simple and uncomplicated. The sound is shallow and weedy, and you can often fish it with only two kinds of lures: topwater or weedless. Usually, all you need to fish Currituck are two lures: a yellow Jitterbug and a Johnson weedless spoon.

"I guess there have been more fish caught on those two lures on Currituck Sound than all the other lures put together," Jimmy Hines once told me. Jimmy grew up on the Outer Banks and had lived on Currituck Sound since retiring from the U.S. Coast Guard some ten years earlier. Like his father-in-law, Wallace O'Neal, Jimmy was a fine hunting and fishing guide.

The Jitterbug and the silver spoon are still probably the favorite lures for fishing the sound. In recent years, the Devils Horse has also become popular.

Tom Ricketson of Clearwater, Florida, fished Currituck in our party several times. Tom, a fine angler, owned plenty of tackle. But he brought very little of it with him. On one trip, he brought only a baitcasting outfit and one lure: a stubby Devils Horse. He clipped off one prong on each of the lure's two treble hooks so that the remaining two prongs rode backwards. That made the hooks semi-weedless. Using only that lure, Tom caught his limit the two days he fished.

When the water is choppy, which is much of the time on the sound, the Devils Horse and other topwater lures should be worked hard enough to kick up a good disturbance. In my mind's ear, I can still hear Wallace O'Neal chiding, "You don't tear up the water enough with that bait!"

When the water is calm or there is only a light ripple, a topwater lure should be worked slowly and gently to make it do a tantalizing dance. Under those conditions, a small lure such as the Tiny Torpedo is extremely effective.

The Jitterbug is often at its best when fished just fast enough to make it gurgle. At other times, the best way to fish the Jitterbug is to toss it out against the marsh, or at the edge of a duck blind, or over the top of a weed bed, and then let it sit a few seconds before retrieving it. Then you pull it about five feet and stop it again. You repeat this stop-and-go motion all the way back to the boat.

When you use a Jitterbug this way, a bass will often slap it before you even start to retrieve it. At other times, you'll get a strike when the lure is moving. Occasionally a bass will hit the lure as you are getting ready to lift it from the water to make another cast. When that happens, the explosion is so great I sometimes think I'm going to have another heart attack.

Most Currituck guides prefer yellow lures. "I don't care what color you use as long as it's yellow" — this has been said so many times by so many guides that it's now a cliche.

When I first started fishing Currituck many years ago, I always took along my regular tackle box. Like most dedicated anglers, I own so much fishing paraphernalia it is a wonder I don't get a hernia just lugging my tackle box to the boat and back. It finally dawned on me that I didn't need all that gear to fish the sound. So I replaced the big tackle box with a small box I dubbed my "Currituck Kit." In addition to such things as first aid and snake bite kits, pliers, screwdriver, extra line, and spare reel parts, I put only a few lures in it.

The lures: two Jitterbugs, one yellow and one black; two Tiny

Torpedoes, one yellow and one black; two baitcasting-size
Shakespeare Brawlers, one a yellow perch color and the other a
home-painted yellow with black spots; two baitcasting-size
Johnson weedless spoons, one silver and one gold; two Number 2
Barracuda weedless Reflecto spoons, both nickel-color; a dozen
fly-rod popping bugs, some yellow and some black. After a couple
of years, I added a few artificial worms to the kit.

The Shakespeare Brawler is a topwater lure that looks like a
Tiny Torpedo, except that the Brawler is made of wood instead of
plastic. I haven't been able to find any new ones in recent years, so
I've carefully nurtured the two that I own, repainting them and
replacing the hooks every year. I like the Brawler so much that I've
made several lures that look like it. The Creek Chub Injured
Minnow is also a good topwater lure for Currituck Sound. The
Hula Popper is another old favorite.

In fact, almost any lure that floats will sometimes catch fish on
Currituck. I remember something that happened while Hubert
Breeze (a colleague on the *Greensboro News & Record*) and I were
fishing the sound one day. Wallace O'Neal, our guide, had pulled
his skiff up to the marsh for us to eat lunch. I reached into my
tackle box for a "popping bug" I had made from a huge cork as a
joke. It had long, gaudy feathers. The hook and cork were so large
that the world's record bass probably couldn't have stretched its
mouth around them. Before preparing to eat, I put the contraption
on the end of a heavy spinning rod and cast to the edge of the
marsh ahead of the skiff. Hubert shook his head. Mr. O'Neal
looked at me as if he felt pity for me. The wind was blowing
slightly, and I put the rod down, leaving the lure to bob on the
water.

I then reached for my lunch box, took out a sandwich and
unwrapped it. Next, I extracted my Thermos bottle, poured a cup of
coffee, and leaned back to enjoy lunch. About five minutes later —
if you don't believe this, ask Hubert — it happened.

We heard a muffled explosion, a noise I imagined sounded like
a shotgun going off under water. We turned and saw a depression
on the water. The cork and metal and feather bug — a thing so ugly
it would have frightened its own mother, if it had a mother — had

disappeared!

I almost fell out of the boat trying to get to my rod. I was too late. We stared incredulously as the waves created by what must have been a monster bass finally disappeared. The water settled back down again to be disturbed only by the wind.

Probably a majority of the big bass caught on the sound over the years have been fooled by the Johnson weedless spoon. Guides usually suggest that the spoon be fished so it darts. But the most bass I've ever seen caught on a Johnson spoon were landed by my friend Tom Fee, who fished it with a fast, steady retrieve. The wind was blowing hard, and the water was low. The fast retrieve forced the lure to run just under the water's surface and over most of the weeds.

Many anglers fish the spoon with a pork strip. I fish it with a Hawaiian Wiggler skirt, turned backwards on the hook. After the invention of artificial worms, Currituck guides discovered that short curly-tailed worms, especially white ones, also made good trailers.

I have good luck with the weedless Barracuda spoon when bass are hitting under water. I bought the spoon at the suggestion of Ralph Clark, a friend who then sold fishing tackle at a hardware store. I stuck the spoon in my tackle box and forgot about it until several Currituck trips later when Hubert Breeze joined our regular group of anglers for the first time. For several months, I had bragged to Hubert about how good fishing on the sound was. As so often happens after you've built a place up, the fishing started off slowly. For about two hours, the only strike we got was when something hit Hubert's artificial worm. We figured it was a chain pickerel (a jack) because the fish bit off the back of the worm.

During the next two hours, we tried about everything in our tackle boxes without getting a hit. Then, as I once more rummaged around in my tackle box, I spotted the Barracuda spoon and tied it on my spinning outfit. On the third cast, I felt a hit. It was a keeper bass. In about an hour, I had my limit on the Barracuda.

That was the only Barracuda spoon we had between us. Feeling very noble, I clipped the spoon off my line and tossed it to Hubert. I jokingly told Mr. O'Neal, our guide, that I had to be nice to

Hubert because Hubert was my boss. That was true; Hubert was then my city editor. But Hubert knew that even if he had owned the newspaper, I wouldn't have given him the spoon if I hadn't already caught my limit.

Within a short time, Hubert caught his limit on the spoon. The rest of the day we swapped the spoon back and forth, releasing the other fish we caught.

Catching bass on the spoon that day was almost as much fun as catching them on a topwater bait. The water was so translucent we could often see the bass hit the spoon.

That was the first time Mr. O'Neal had seen a Barracuda spoon. He was so impressed that I sent him several after I got back to Greensboro. When he wrote to thank me, he said, "I had a party out today, and they used the spoons you sent. They caught their limits in a little hole, and I didn't even have to move the boat."

I received another note about that fishing trip. Hubert wrote: "Currituck was everything you said it was and more. Thanks."

The plastic worm was slow to catch on at Currituck Sound. I don't why, because it is an ideal lure for the sound. Bill Black, one of the best anglers I know, caught some of the biggest bass in our fishing parties while using the worm. Bill sometimes used a worm, rigged "Texas style," but without any weight. That made the worm weedless, and it crawled right over the grass. It was so fascinating to watch Bill use the worm that I often forgot to make casts. The bass would sometimes swirl at the worm three or four times before engulfing it. And Bill lost few fish. He set the hook so hard, he rocked the boat.

Like most other good anglers, Bill experimented when the fish ignored the traditional Currituck lures. He caught a lot of fish on spinner baits and on Mepps-type spinners decorated with a strip of pork rind. He almost always caught one of the biggest fish in our parties of eight or ten fishermen.

On some days, you can catch fish on Currituck no matter what kind of bait you use. I remember one trip when Dr. Richard Whitaker of Kernersville and his nephew, Frank Whitaker of Oak Ridge, stayed at the same fishing lodge where our party was staying. It was fun to listen to Dr. Whitaker recount his fishing experiences. He had fished Currituck for many years. One morning out on the sound, Jack Watson and I saw Frank and Dr. Whitaker with Booty Spruill, a well-known guide. While Jack and I watched, the Whitakers caught and released five or six bass on their fly rods in just a few minutes.

"Well, I did something this morning I've never done before," Dr. Whitaker said at dinner that night. "Booty took some live minnows out, and we caught our limits in about an hour. We had already caught our limits when we saw you. Then we switched to fly rods and caught fish on them, too."

I remember many other Currituck trips when the bass were not especially particular about what they hit. One was in mid-May when Charlie Reid, then a Greensboro banker, made his second trip with our group. Charlie's first trip had not been successful. A strong nor'easter almost blew us off the sound.

On the drive back from that first trip — the one when we caught only a few fish — Charlie and I got into a friendly argument. Charlie, who grew up in Charlotte, said he thought the famous Santee-Cooper lakes in South Carolina offered a better place to fish for bass than Currituck. I disagreed, of course.

The next trip to Currituck changed Charlie's mind. Everybody in our party of eight caught a limit of bass. The bass hit popping bugs. They hit underwater spoons. They hit topwater lures. They hit artificial worms. All you had to do was get a lure close to a bass, and the bass would attack it.

Andrew Lewis, then a young Pennsylvanian, was on that trip. Drew, who was later to become President Reagan's secretary of transportation, had hunted and fished all over the country, but said he had never seen such good bass fishing as on Currituck Sound.

In fact, the fishing there is so good that Jack VanAlst declared he would never go back to Currituck again. "The fishing was so sensational that I'm afraid I would be disappointed if I went back and didn't have that kind of luck," said the Greensboro banker. "I'd like to remember Currituck the rest of my life the way it was on that trip."

You can catch fish on Currituck Sound with any kind of tackle. I usually carry three rigged outfits: a baitcasting rod loaded with 20-pound line, an open-face spinning outfit loaded with 8-pound test line, and a fly rod with a Number 8 or 9 bug-tapered line.

I also now carry a spare fly rod. I learned that lesson the hard way while fishing Currituck with my older son, John Gerard. It was early June, but the heat was heavy on the first day of our trip. That would have been bearable if the fishing had been good. But we didn't get a single roll the first day.

The next morning, however, a light refreshing rain began to fall as we were eating breakfast and continued all day. Our guide took us to a creek where we saw bass swirling all around. Within 15 minutes, I caught four bass, all larger than the average Currituck bass. John Gerard hooked and landed one bass on a Tiny Torpedo. Then I hooked a bass that weighed no more than two pounds. He jumped and threw the bug. When I started to make another cast, about six inches of the tip of my rod broke off. We couldn't repair it, and I didn't have a spare.

Although we caught other fish that day with spinning tackle, the fishing was not as good as it had been with the fly rod. That's why I always carry a spare with me now, no matter where I'm fishing.

Every guide I know agrees that on most days, a fly rod will catch more fish on Currituck Sound than any other type of tackle. Medium-size popping bugs in yellow are favored by guides. But just about any color popping bug will catch bass at times. Black is especially good on dark days.

One reason the fly rod is so good on Currituck is that it's ideal for fishing the aquatic grass. You can drop the bug into a small opening in the grass, twitch it several times, lift it out, and cast it to another hole — all without getting hung on the grass. The fact that Currituck is shallow in most places also makes the popping bug an ideal lure for the sound.

Most years, the popping bug and other topwater lures are good lures to use from mid-spring through summer and into late fall.

Many people who regularly fish Currituck think spring is the best time to fish the sound. However, I have caught more fish and bigger fish in September, October, and early November than during any other time. Admittedly, the weather is more uncertain in the fall when the hurricane season is in full bloom. The sound can be balmy and calm one hour, and cold and blustery the next.

Bill Jerome, a Greensboro neighbor, had an experience with me one fall that I will never forget. Early in the morning, the sound was so still that I had no trouble using a fly rod. But then the wind began blowing so hard that we couldn't even cast spoons on baitcasting rods. That's what caused me to hook our fishing guide, Wallace O'Neal.

One of the lure's two treble hooks pierced Mr. O'Neal's right ear lobe. Hanging out of Mr. O'Neal's ear, the colorful lure looked like an Ubanga warrior's earring. First-aid manuals say the best way to remove a hook is to push the barb on through the flesh, snip off the barb, and then back out the hook. But the hook was imbedded at such an odd angle in Mr. O'Neal's ear that Bill and I were afraid to try that.

"Just jerk it out then," Mr. O'Neal growled.

I refused. Bill and I got the screws off the lure so the hook was the only thing left in Mr. O'Neal's ear. I insisted we return to the hunting and fishing lodge, get an automobile, and go to a doctor.

"Well," Mr. O'Neal said, "why don't we fish this little bit of marsh right here before we go in?"

I looked out across the open sound and realized why Mr. O'Neal was reluctant to go in. The sound was boiling with whitecaps.

We finally persuaded him to go. But he declined to let me run his boat, saying, "I'm more use to it."

The ride across the sound was the roughest I ever experienced. One minute we'd be on top of a wave with a spectacular view of the sound; the next minute the boat would drop with a bone-jarring thud, and we'd land in a trough between waves so high that all we could see around us were walls of water. Mr. O'Neal had to pull the plug in the bottom of the skiff so the water would run out and keep the boat from swamping. He zig-zagged across the sound to avoid taking the waves straight on. Even though we wore rain gear, the spray soaked us. All the time, the treble hook swung back and forth in Mr. O'Neal's ear.

"Have you ever turned over a boat out here?" I yelled to the old fishing guide.

"No," he shouted back, "and I don't intend to start now."

Bill and I breathed a little easier.

After we safely made our way across the sound and found a doctor, the doc sprayed Mr. O'Neal's ear with Novocaine and removed the hook.

The next morning dawned fair, calm — and cold. Jimmie Jeffries, a photographer who was in our group, put his coat over his head, dashed out into the yard to look at a thermometer, ran back inside, and announced that the temperature was 24 degrees Fahrenheit. Nevertheless, Mr. O'Neal showed up after breakfast, ready to go fishing. He said his ear didn't hurt. "My daughter said if I ever wanted to start wearing an earring, my ear is already pierced," he laughed.

Unfortunately, we had brought only light clothes. We were so cold after an hour of fishing that we decided to quit and drive home. It was really raw, which helps explain why few people fish Currituck in the winter. During cold weather, most anglers leave the sound to duck hunters and commercial netters.

But when the fall weather is good on Currituck, it is the most pleasant time of the year. The air is so pure and crisp it's intoxicating. The duck and Canada geese are just beginning to return, and fall wildflowers are in full bloom. You feel that all is right with the world.

Currituck Sound also has the biggest concentration of Eurasian milfoil, an aquatic grass, of any body of water in North Carolina. The grass is a good example of how man can change his environment for good or bad.

Milfoil was imported into the United States from the Orient and was first sold for use in tropical fish aquariums. In this country, it apparently was first grown by entrepreneurs in New England and was gradually transported south by ducks and geese. It thrives in brackish water, and the first heavy concentration south of the Mason-Dixon line was in Baltimore Harbor. It finally choked itself out there.

In my opinion, milfoil has helped the fishing on Currituck

Sound. Many people feel differently, however. One of the state's best-known sportsmen, Hargrove "Skipper" Bowles, started fishing Currituck in the early 1940s, long before the first sprig of milfoil appeared. "There is no doubt in my mind," he declared. "We caught more bass and larger bass then."

Skipper was former head of the N.C. Department of Conservation and Development, now the Department of Economic and Natural Resources. The department has studied the milfoil from time to time to decide what, if anything, should be done about it.

Milfoil or no milfoil, Skipper said Currituck was still the best place in the world to fish for largemouth bass. And he had fished all over the world. "You'll get more action in Currituck than any other place," he said.

John Kent Davis, on the other hand, disliked the milfoil so much that he quit fishing Currituck. Like Skipper, he too had fished the sound since the early 1940s. "Before the milfoil, the sound was so clear in places that you could fish a Mepps spinner without getting hung up," John Kent recalled. "In fact, that was my favorite lure on Currituck Sound."

Another friend, Jack Watson, fished Currituck for many years before the milfoil took over, but then quit fishing the sound for awhile. Then, some time after the milfoil had gained a strong hold, Jack joined our regular twice-a-year expedition to the sound. He was in a good position to see the difference the milfoil made. "It seems to me that the fishing was much better before the milfoil," Jack said.

Roger Soles, who began fishing the sound in the mid-1940s, took a different view. "I believe there are probably more fish in the sound than there ever were," he said. "But it's harder to catch them now. I think there may be more large fish now than there were. I know I've caught bigger fish in recent years."

Roger, a good bass fly-rod angler, said he thought the cover provided by the milfoil helped the fish population. Many professional guides agreed with that.

I believe it, too. When I began fishing Currituck in the early 1960s, a bass over five pounds was rare. Now it is not. Beginning about 1970, at least one person in our group of eight to ten anglers usually caught at least one bass that weighed over six pounds. I have caught, while using a fly rod, several bass that weighed more than six pounds. On one trip, I landed two six-and-a-half-pounders on a fly rod.

The main objection to the milfoil is that it sometimes takes the fight out of the bass. They often dive into the milfoil after they're hooked, forcing you to dig them out with a landing net. You lose some nice fish that way.

When the water is high, you can prevent the fish from getting into the milfoil by holding your rod high while playing the fish. Also, you can often flush a bass that is tangled in the milfoil by holding your line tight and tapping on the butt of your rod. This sends vibrations down through the line.

Fortunately, milfoil doesn't hang your lure so tightly that you have to go after it. You can free a lure by pulling hard. But then you usually have to reel in the line and pick off the milfoil before making another cast.

Nevertheless, most knowledgeable anglers rank Currituck Sound as one of the top bass fishing spots in the world. Arnie Culbreth of Greensboro, a fisherman all his life, went to Currituck with us one time — his first trip to the sound. Four of us got down early enough to fish a few hours in the afternoon on the first day. Arnie and I fished together those few hours, and Wallace O'Neal, our guide, stopped the boat about 100 yards from the marsh. It looked as if we were fishing too far out from shore.

"I've had real good luck here lately," Mr. O'Neal said. "There's a grass bed right under us. Just cast out all around the boat."

Arnie fished a Devils Toothpick. I used my fly rod and a medium-size popping bug. There was plenty of water in the sound and it covered the grass bed. Within two hours, Arnie and I both caught our limits. Arnie said he had never seen fishing that good.

Hugh Page, who was then a newspaper colleague, caught his limit of bass in Currituck the second time he had ever been bass fishing in his life. Another friend, Glenn Mays, said after his first day on the sound, "I've never seen fishing anywhere as good as it was the first day." Glenn, then a bachelor, had fished all over the

Piedmont and western North Carolina.

Everybody in our group caught his limit on that first day. Unfortunately, a weather front moved in the second day, and the cold rain and wind it brought forced us to quit fishing.

Ralph Bazhaw, a friend who has enough Potawatomi Indian blood in his veins to be carried on the tribal rolls in Oklahoma, substituted for a last-minute dropout on one of our Currituck trips. Although he now lives in Greensboro, he had fished all over the country. The fishing was so good on that trip that he became a regular member of our Currituck group. "It is the most consistent place I have ever fished," he said.

There are several hunting and fishing lodges and motels on Currituck Sound. You can find more luxurious accommodations on the Outer Banks. A partial listing of accommodations is carried in a directory published by the N.C. Travel Division. No matter where you stay, you should make reservations as far in advance of your trip as possible.

Currituck hunting and fishing lodges usually serve breakfast and dinner and pack a lunch for you to take out on the sound. But when you make reservations, you check on this to make sure. In general, the hospitality and food at the lodges are superb.

Nags Head, an Outer Banks beach community, is only a few miles' drive from Currituck. If you stay there, you have the option of renting a motel room with a kitchenette, and you can commute to the sound each day.

Most of the lodges and motels on Currituck will book a guide for you if you ask them far enough in advance of your trip. Like most people in eastern North Carolina, the guides are obliging and friendly. It would be unwise to fish Currituck without a guide unless you are thoroughly familiar with the sound.

Currituck Sound received a deluge of publicity after a national bass tournament was held there a few years back. The professional anglers who fished the tournament launched their boats on Albemarle Sound, however, and few of them fished on Currituck; they fished other tributaries of Albemarle Sound instead. But they did get a taste of how violent the weather can be along that stretch of the North Carolina coast. At least one boat was smashed when it was blown against a dock.

Even veterans of the sound get into trouble if they get caught in a fog without a compass. Fog can roll in with frightening swiftness, blotting out the sun and all landmarks. The fog is sometimes so thick that your partner, sitting just a few feet away, appears ghost-like. A world that was filled with sunshine just a few minutes earlier can suddenly become white and unreal.

I can tolerate the fog; I know it will lift sooner or later. But when the guide is feeling his way through the thick mist and I hear a roll of thunder — even if it's far away — I get jittery. I've had a near-psychotic fear of lightning on the water ever since Roger Soles and I were caught, along with a guide, in a spectacular thunderstorm. (If you've never experienced a North Carolina thunderstorm at close hand, you may not be prepared for its vio-lence.) Time after time, lightning blasted the marsh not more than 20 yards away. The strikes were so close that we smelled ozone in the air and felt the boat shudder. I hadn't been so scared since the Korean War.

Now, when there is the slightest hint of an electrical storm, I tell the guide to get ready to make a run home — even though I know I'll get a lot of razzing from my fishing friends that night. But it's better to be safe than sorry. There are very few shelters on Currituck Sound's eastern marshes, so you are often the tallest object around — making you a good target for lightning.

There are other hazards to be aware of, too. Greensboro pho-tographer Carol Martin had fished Currituck in his own boat for years, and he knew the sound about as well as he knew the inside of his darkroom. Yet he and his son-in-law, Larry Moser, got caught in a fog one day. They had to spend the entire night on the marsh. If you've ever seen the huge, poisonous cottonmouth water moccasins that infest the Currituck marshes, you'll understand why Carol swore he would never again fish Currituck without a com-pass.

Not only did Carol and Larry have to spend the night on the marsh, but the wind blew so hard during the night that their boat sank. Even after the fog lifted the next morning, they were still stranded.

All night, U.S. Coast Guardsmen using powerful searchlights had hunted fruitlessly for Carol and Larry. Finally, at about 10 o'clock the next morning, Currituck resident Captain Walt Perry (the title "Captain" was honorary but deserved) guessed where the wind must have blown the lost fishermen. "He went right to them," recalled Dave Goforth, who was in the fishing party with Larry and Carol.

J.T. Hunter and Roger Blackwood, who also were in the fishing party, were more lucky. At about midnight, they hit a spot of land they knew. They pulled their boat to shore and walked out of the swamp.

"I was the only one in the group who had a compass on my boat," Hunter Galloway said. "You'd better believe that the next time we went fishing, everybody had a compass on his boat."

Carson Bain and Bill Sullivan, two veteran Currituck anglers, also managed to find their way home that day — with some good navigation and a little luck. "Unless you know the water, you're far better to use a guide," Bill later declared. "I fished it for years with a guide before I started fishing it on my own. And if you're not well-equipped with a good boat and a good compass, you're taking a lot of risk because of the sudden squalls and fogs that can blow in. The water is shallow, which adds to the risk."

Carson agreed. "I went for 20 years with a guide before I ever attempted to fish it on my own," he said. "I've seen people wear out a propeller blade trying to get out of the mud when they were within a few feet of a channel."

Some people wade the sound. But Carson said he wouldn't. "There are too many cottonmouths."

Carson said he used the "buddy system" — fishing within shouting distance of friends in another boat — whenever possible. "It's easy to get lost unless you really know what you're doing. The sound changes dramatically from year to year, or even from month to month."

Periodic burning of the marshes, for example, changes their appearance.

Carson once found his way out of a Currituck pond during a

fog by using an unorthodox system of navigation. When Carson told his partner he knew where he was, his partner asked how he knew. "Because this is the only place on the sound where the bottom is like it is here," Carson replied as he peered at the water.

Carson, Bill Sullivan, Dave Goforth, and some of their friends now know the sound so well that even the professional guides respect them. That is quite a compliment. Guides often laugh at what they refer to as "do-it-yourselfers."

Another reason for fishing with a guide at least once is that they make good companions. They usually have a wry sense of humor and help make a day fun even when the fishing is poor. Also, a guide furnishes the boat, motor, and gasoline. Some bring along extra lures in case you don't have the proper ones yourself. But Currituck guides don't usually fish for themselves while guiding; they're too busy poling the boat for you. The standard guide's fee, like everything else, increases every few years. Most people tip their guides.

If you insist on fishing Currituck on your own, you need a powerful electric motor, preferably one that is foot-controlled. You should have a weed guard on the motor. And, of course, you need a reliable outboard motor.

I fished Currituck about 20 times before I gained enough confidence to fish the sound in my own 14-foot aluminum boat. I still prefer to fish with a guide, but I have had some good days of fishing in my own boat.

When my sons go with me to Currituck, I usually take my own boat. Guides' fees are now relatively expensive if you're paying for two people. Besides, I enjoy being alone with my sons. We've caught a lot of fish while fishing on our own.

Clark White, a Greensboro friend, was with me the second time I ever fished Currituck in my boat. The first day, a driving rain and high winds curtailed our fishing, but we still caught a few fish. I caught a five-pounder on my fly rod, which was worth the trip, especially because I caught it in open water. The bass made several beautiful jumps before Clark got the landing net under it.

The second day, the weather improved. Even though we fished only half a day, we caught at least 50 bass. Most of them were small, but we had our limits of keepers before noon. Clark said it was the best bass fishing he had ever experienced.

There has always been salt in Currituck Sound. But during the drought years of the mid-1980s, some people began to worry that the salt in Currituck's water had increased to the point where it had hurt the bass fishing. For the first time since I began fishing Currituck a quarter-century before, it became difficult to catch a limit of bass in a day's time.

Fisheries biologist Pete Kornegay said he thought rainfall patterns would have to return to normal before fishing returned to normal. Mr. Kornegay is the fisheries biologist for the N.C. Wildlife Resources Commission for the district that covers Currituck Sound.

I hope that Currituck fishing won't become just a fond memory. During most of the years I've fished the sound, it has been one of the best places in the world to catch bass.

North River
And
Collington

When The Wind Blows On Currituck

Bill Keys and I had pulled my boat out of the water on the North
River and were securing our gear for the ride back to the motel
when Dave Goforth's boat chugged up to the landing. We spoke to
Dave.

"You know this man?" Dave asked, nodding in the direction
of his partner.

Of course we knew Dave's partner. He was wearing the same
style hat that had, along with his famous golf swing, made him
famous to several generations of sports fans. It was Sam Snead, the
professional golfer.

I asked if they had caught anything. Sam hoisted a beautiful
string of white perch, yellow perch, bream, flounder, largemouth
bass, and chain pickerel (or "jack") out of the water.

Now, Sam and Dave had not journeyed to the northeast corner
of North Carolina to fish the North River. Neither had Bill and I.
We had all come to fish Currituck Sound. But that morning, when
the sun peeped up, a nor'easter was whipping Currituck into a mass
of whitecaps. The water on the sound was so low that it would have
been nearly impossible to fish, even if the sound had been placid.
Conditions were so bad that even the professional guides had
decided stay in and forego a day's pay.

I suggested to Bill that we fish the North River, which is only a
15-minute drive from the motel on Currituck Sound where we were
staying. The North River can often save the day after you've made
the long, hard drive across the state only to find you can't fish the
sound because of high winds. Most of the time, you can fish the

river even when Currituck is too rough to fish.

The North River certainly saved this day, at least for Sam Snead and Dave Goforth, as well as for Bill and me.

Nobody seems to know for certain why strong northeast winds affect the North River less than they affect Currituck. One reason may be that parts of the river are more sheltered than Currituck.

Dave Goforth's theory is that there are more creeks and deep spots on the North River than on Currituck Sound, so there are places to fish even when the water is low. Day in and day out, however, the bass fishing on the North River will not compare with the fishing on Currituck Sound. Nevertheless, North River fishing is often sensational when compared to most other places.

One of the prettiest strings of bass I have ever seen came out of the North River. They were caught by my friends Woody Tilley, a Greensboro lawyer, and Dr. Bob Harned, a Greensboro dentist. Woody caught the largest ones on an artificial worm fished with weedless hooks and no weight. The worm worked its way down through the grass as if it were alive. Bob caught most of his on a fly rod.

The Intracoastal Waterway links the North River to Currituck Sound, and in places the two bodies of water are similar. In some sections, the North River has marshlands. In those areas, you would think you were on Currituck Sound if you didn't know better. And where the river is open, it can get rough in a blow, just like the sound.

But in other spots, the North River looks more like what it really is: a river. In these reaches, it is sheltered by trees and is placid. Water lilies grow in some pockets.

The day Bill Keys and I met Dave Goforth and Sam Snead, Bill got strike after strike as he crawled a black Johnson spoon across a bed of lily pads at a creek mouth on the river. True, Bill didn't catch many of the bass that blew holes through the lily pads trying to get to his lure; but he did get the ones that nailed the spoon just as it dropped off the edges of the lily pads.

I didn't have a spoon the same size and color as Bill's, and I couldn't get a strike when I tried fishing my other spoons exactly the way Bill fished his. It was frustrating.

Later in the day, we returned to the same creek, and I picked up a few bass on a topwater lure and on a fly-rod popping bug.

In most places, the North River is easier to fish on your own than is Currituck. Still, you need a stable boat. The day Bob Harned and Woody Tilley caught that pretty string of fish, they learned about that. During the morning, we all crossed the river to fish the creeks on the west side. The river was so rough coming back that Van King and I had to zig-zag to avoid taking big waves head on. Back in the creek, close to the boat landing, however, the water was calm. That was where Woody and Bob caught their bass.

You also need to watch your landmarks closely while fishing the North River. You can get lost. Some days, you can fish all day long in the ponds and creeks off the main channel of the river and not see another person to ask for help. If you don't have a boat or feel uncertain about fishing the North River on your own, there are a few guides who specialize in North River fishing.

If you do fish the North River without a guide, be sure you take a map and a compass. Although the main channel is well marked — a concession to the Intracoastal Waterway traffic — there are no markers where you often find the best fishing. Also, milfoil grass has attacked the North River in some sections and it can be a nuisance. Be careful to clear your outboard motor when you notice the boat slowing to a crawl because of the grass.

In most places, you fish the North River using the same methods you use on Currituck. But in a few places, especially around the mouths of creeks and on some stretches of the main body of the river, you can use Rapalas, Rebels, Mepps spinners, and other non-weedless lures. But hold onto your rod, especially when using Rapalas and Rebels. Every now and then, you'll get a jolt that will make you think you've caught a world-record large-mouth bass. The North River has some big striped bass.

Sam Snead and Dave Goforth had been using some of the lures Dave makes when they caught that string of fish on the North River. Dave enjoys fishing the river because he likes to catch all kinds of fish, not just bass. The river is better than Currituck Sound for that.

If you fish the North River in your own boat, there are several places you can launch. One is the N.C. Wildlife Resources Commission landing near Waterlily. Then you make a run down the Intracoastal Waterway under the Coinjock bridge on Highway 158 to reach the North River. But it is nearer to the good fishing to launch your boat at a commercial landing on the west side of the bridge, even though it'll cost you a little money.

My favorite place to launch is behind the Riveria Hunting and Fishing Lodge. You have to pay a small fee to launch there, unless you are staying at the lodge. But it is nearer to what usually is the best fishing than the other landings. A canal leads from the Riveria landing to the river.

There are a lot of snags and floating debris in the canal, so you should be careful. Hubert Breeze and I broke a shear pin on our outboard motor the first time we fished that part of the river. Once you get out of the canal, though, you can start fishing immediately.

I will long remember the September weekend I first fished the North River. I didn't own a boat then, so I borrowed my dad's. Hubert Breeze and I arranged to meet Claibourne Darden and Bynum Hines, who were to fish in Claibourne's boat, at a motel on Currituck Sound. But one look at the wind-swept sound convinced us we should fish the North River. Claibourne had fished it before and knew where to go.

After an agreeable morning of fishing on the river, Claibourne found a spot on the bank that was dry enough for us to get out of our boats without miring up. "I believe this is a good place for us to cook lunch," he said after signaling for us to pull our boat alongside his.

Stately pine trees and undergrowth sheltered the spot. As we stepped from our boats, a big, beautiful buck deer bounded off into the thicket. He must have been lying in the shade a long time. His bed was still warm to the touch.

After one of Claibourne's delicious dinners of fresh fish and hush puppies, not to mention Bynum's slaw, we leaned back against the trees, sipped hot coffee, and enjoyed the scenery and the feeling of euphoria that full bellies bring. We were on the main body of water and could see the passing parade of yachts bound for Florida on the Intracoastal Waterway. Some of the yachts slowed when they spotted our tiny skiffs pulled up on shore. The pilots signaled, asking if we needed help. We waved them on.

When one particularly large and luxurious yacht passed, Bynum remarked, "I'd sure like to be doing that."

"Bynum," I chided, "I bet they are not having any more fun than we are."

"I meant I'd like to do that if I didn't have this to do," Bynum answered in a sincere tone.

COLLINGTON AND KITTY HAWK

There are several other good places to fish for bass within easy driving distance of Currituck Sound. The best-known are Collington and Kitty Hawk Bay. These two bodies of water are close together and offer excellent fishing. They are about 12 miles south of the lower reaches of Currituck Sound and are just west of the Outer Banks beach community of Kill Devil Hills on Albemarle Sound. Both can be reached from the N.C. Wildlife Resources Commission landing at Avalon Beach west of Highway 158. There are other boat launching areas behind the Wright Brothers Memorial, a tall granite obelisk that's hard to miss almost anywhere on the upper Outer Banks.

This water is a little easier to fish on your own than is Currituck Sound — but not much. You should hire a guide at least the first few times you fish it. The water can turn violent in a high wind, and to make matters worse, you could get lost. Like much of the rest of the water in this part of the state, one place looks much like another to the inexperienced eye. Also, be careful not to get your motor entangled; there is some milfoil grass in Kitty Hawk Bay and in the creeks and ponds of Collington.

Use the same methods of fishing this area that you'd use on Currituck. It is particularly good fly-rod water.

You can choose from a wide variety of motels, hotels, and fine restaurants along this popular stretch of the Outer Banks. Because the area was so remote from the rest of the state until recent years, the local people are largely unspoiled. The older ones still speak the Elizabethan English of their forefathers, a pretty, musical-like dialect in which *guide* and *tide* are pronounced *guoyide* and *tuoyide*. Like the water you'll be fishing, the language has just a hint of salt.

Just as on Currituck Sound and the North River, the few people who still make their living as guides are great companions, so it's worth your money to share some of their philosophy. You will have plenty of time to fish the area on your own after you get to know it better.

The Pungo And Tributaries

Chapter 9

Freshwater Bass And Saltwater Species
— All For The Price Of One

Bass fishing is an obsession with many anglers. They don't like it when something other than a bass wallops their lures. But some people enjoy the mystery of not knowing what kind of fish will hit their lures next. Happily, there are places in North Carolina where you can catch bass and other species of fish on the same lures and in the same water.

The Pungo River area is one of the most interesting of these places. It offers some fine largemouth bass fishing, but you should also be prepared to sometimes catch other fish — both freshwater and saltwater varieties.

The most dramatic example of this kind of fishing I ever witnessed was on Back Creek near Bath. My fishing buddy Bill Black, using an ultralight spinning rod and a small jig with a strip of cut fish, caught more than half a dozen species of fish, including bass. On one of his first casts, he hooked what obviously was a strong fish.

"It must be a striped bass," I said as I waited with the landing net during Bill's two-minute struggle with the fish. When Bill finally worked the fish to the net, we saw it was a puppy drum that weighed about six pounds.

Bill caught four or five other puppy drum on that day. He also caught some bream, croaker, flounder, white perch, yellow perch, and largemouth bass. And he caught them all while I stubbornly continued to whip my fly rod, catching only a few small bass.

Another unusual thing happened to us on that trip. The day

87

after Bill caught all those fish, we fished other rivers and creeks around Belhaven with only moderate success. Remembering how good the fishing was in Back Creek, we stopped there on the way home the next day and caught a few more fish. As we were taking our boat out of the water, we met a husband and wife who had fished the creek during the morning.

"Have any luck?" I asked.

"We had a lovely morning," the woman replied.

I looked in their live well. They had two large bass and a nice puppy drum. The husband said he and his wife had caught all the fish on artificial worms.

I introduced myself. The wife opened the door of their four-wheel drive car and rushed back to where I was standing. At first, I thought I had said something to offend her. But then I saw her nice smile.

"Why, Buck Paysour!" she cried. "You're the reason we're living down here."

I wondered how I could have been responsible for that; I had never even met them before. The woman introduced herself as Louise Kidd and her husband as Rollie Kidd. Rollie was an engineer, and Louise a schoolteacher. Louise explained that she and Rollie lived in Morganton (in western North Carolina) when they read the first edition of *Bass Fishing in North Carolina*. They were so intrigued by what I wrote about the Pungo that they visited the area to see for themselves. They liked it so much they later moved to Washington, N.C.

After I met the Kidds, I often telephoned them to check on fishing in the area. We developed a close friendship over the telephone. But for some reason, I once missed calling them for about six months. The next time I called, I was shocked and saddened to learn that Rollie had died of cancer.

The Pungo River and nearby streams and their tributaries are basically freshwater streams. The water, however, has just enough salt to support many species of saltwater and migratory fish. These include such fish as flounder, croaker, bluefish, puppy drum, striped bass, and spotted and gray seatrout. It is a narrow-minded bass angler indeed who doesn't get a kick out of occasionally landing one of these species.

At times, you may see more exotic species of marine life in the Pungo River. Dave Goforth, one of the state's best all-around anglers, used to see porpoises in the same water in which he caught largemouth bass.

Curtis Youngblood and I once saw what we thought was a huge tarpon — it must have weighed 100 pounds — come out of the water on Pungo Creek. The big fish jumped clear of the water within sight of where Curtis, James A. King Sr., Aubrey Edwards, and I had caught our limits of largemouth bass a day earlier.

But don't worry. If you insist on fishing exclusively for bass, you can catch mostly bass in this water if you use the right kinds of lures. You'll have to put up with only an occasional hit from something else.

If, on the other hand, you enjoy surprises and variety in your fishing, you can arrange that, too, by using lures that will catch bass and other fish as well.

My friends Claibourne Darden and John Peterson became experts on "mixed-bag fishing" on the Pungo. For 20 years or more, they made several trips a year to the area. When the weather turned bad, they spent their time driving around exploring for new water to fish. While preferring to catch largemouth bass on fly rods, Claibourne and John never felt too noble to switch tackle and fish for something else when the bass ignored their popping bugs. They discovered that the best producers for mixed-bag fishing included natural baits and such lures as Rebels and Rapalas, Mepps spinners with pork rinds, Beetle spins and similar lures, and "fat" lures such as the Big O. When using these lures, especially in the smaller sizes, they not only caught bass, but also jack, bream, yellow perch, white perch, an occasional striped bass, and several species of saltwater fish.

I once fished the Pungo with Claibourne. I was too stubborn to put down my fly rod even after Claibourne had switched to frozen shrimp. He fished the shrimp with a small cork on a spinning reel. Fishing the rig shallow, casting to the edge of the marsh, he caught largemouth bass and several other varieties of fish, including some of the biggest yellow perch I had ever seen. The perch were larger than the few bass I caught on my fly rod.

John Baskerville, perhaps one of the state's best all-around fly-rod anglers, generally uses the long rod whether he is fishing for brown trout in the mountains or seatrout on the Pungo River. He fishes both topwater bugs and underwater streamers on the Pungo. It takes a lot of skill to fish heavy underwater streamers on the fly rod. But if I were as good as John, that's all I would use. He has even caught puppy drum on his fly rod. Can you imagine such great sport?

On a fall trip to the Pungo, Henry Reeves and Howard Carr used spinning and casting tackle to catch both largemouth bass and seatrout on the same lures and in the same water. John Ellison and I hung and lost several bluefish and striped bass off the same clump of marsh grass on Scranton Creek, a tributary to the Pungo River. A few minutes later, I picked up my fly rod and caught a 6.5-pound largemouth.

Once on Mill Creek, a tributary to Pungo Creek, I hooked a small bass which promptly jumped and threw my fly-rod popping bug. I hadn't moved the boat a foot when Curtis Youngblood caught a nice puppy drum on a Rebel lure.

Spring is probably the best time to fish the Pungo for bass. Fall bass fishing is good, too, and that's when you are most likely to catch many other kinds of fish along with bass. During good years on the Pungo and the creeks that flow into it, the bass start to hit topwater lures early in the spring and continue to hit on top all through the summer and into fall, as late as Thanksgiving. The fly rod is especially potent, but the bass will hit almost any type of topwater bait.

One November morning, Doris Dale and I caught bass after bass on topwater lures while fishing Scranton Creek during a cold rain. Doris Dale used a black Jitterbug. She also caught several small striped bass on a gold-colored Rebel. I caught my largemouth on a black fly-rod popper.

"Tell me again how much fun we're having," Doris Dale said after we had fished about three hours.

I turned and looked at her. She was shivering, and her lips were blue. "Reel in," I said as I cranked the outboard motor and headed for the boat landing. We drove back to Greensboro, where it was so cold we had to scrape ice off the automobile windows the next morning.

In addition to the fly-rod bass bug, other good topwater lures for fishing the Pungo include the Tiny Torpedo, Devils Horse, and similar lures. Most of the time, small topwater lures work best. On good days, you can catch bass on almost any kind and size of surface lure.

With lures such as the Rapala, Rebel, or Bang-O-Lure, the light colors are usually best. These lures are very good for largemouth bass when the fish are in the mood to hit on or just below the surface. When you use them in the spring and fall, hold onto your rod — you might find yourself battling a big striped bass.

I caught my first striped bass one fall while fishing Pantego Creek, a tributary to the Pungo River. Neil Daniels and I had fished one whole day for largemouth bass without getting a strike. The next morning, I flipped a Rebel to some stumps. As soon as I began my retrieve, I felt a jolt from what I first thought was a largemouth bass that weighed at least nine pounds. Then the fish rolled in the clear water, and I saw its stripes. I realized I had hooked my first striper. The water magnified the fish and I guessed it would go 12 pounds. It fought like it, too.

It took me more than five minutes to land the striper on my ultralight spinning rod and four-pound test line. Actually, the fish weighed only a little more than five pounds.

In Mepps spinners, the gold- and silver-bladed medium to small lures are excellent baits. Dave Goforth's Meatgetter spinners are also good, as are the Beetle Spin and Mr. Twister spinners in the smaller sizes. The plastic worm is also a good producer on the Pungo. Most of the time, the six-inch or smaller worms work best. The worm should be rigged "Texas-style" and fished with the smallest weight you can throw. The color of the worm does not seem to make a lot of difference. But be sure to carry a good supply of worms. You lose a lot of them to the crabs and the toothy chain pickerel or "jack" that are plentiful in the Pungo.

There is some farming along the Pungo, so parts of the river get muddy with runoff more quickly than most other coastal-area waters. Also, some of the creeks have been dredged.

Pungo Creek, one of my favorite creeks, gets dingy or even muddy in its upper reaches during a hard rain. When it gets red, you might as well look for another place to fish. When it is clear, it is easy to fish its sheltered upper reaches. Some people fish from tiny one-person boats around the islands that dot the creek.

For a fee, you can launch your boat at a store on the north side of Highway 264 near the bridge at Yeatsville. You might have some difficulty putting in a large boat there, however.

After launching your boat, you go out a canal — slowly, very slowly — until you reach the creek. Then turn left and go under the bridge. You should start fishing just as soon as you clear the bridge. When the bass are hitting, you can catch fish just about any place in the creek.

On most days, if you don't catch fish on Pungo Creek within an hour, you might as well haul out your boat and go somewhere else. There are plenty of other places to try your luck, all within 20 miles of Belhaven.

Pungo Creek can also be good nearer where it empties into the Pungo River. The creek is fairly wide here. If you have a boat that is too large to be launched anywhere but on a good paved landing, you can put in at the Cee-Bee Marina on Highway 92. If you're after largemouth bass exclusively, it is better to fish upstream rather than toward the river. Otherwise, you are more likely to catch seatrout and other saltwater fish. To fish upstream, go out of the canal from the marina, turn right, and then go under the bridge on Highway 92. You can fish for about ten miles before running out of good water.

Pantego Creek is another excellent stream to fish in this area. There are several places to launch your boat, but the most convenient is a marina in Belhaven at the Pantego Creek bridge on Highway 92. The ramps there can accommodate almost any size fishing boat. The best fishing is west of the bridge. Pantego Creek is wide at the bridge, but there are a number of smaller streams that feed into the creek west of the bridge. You can find some shelter from the wind by going into the smaller creeks and sloughs.

Fishing on Pungo Creek itself is often good. One of the easiest places to fish is in the upper stretches of the river. You launch your boat at a landing at Leechville on Highway 264 at the Pungo River Bridge. The fishing is good on both sides of the bridge.

If you get out of the river channel on the west side of the bridge, however, you might have some trouble. Not only is it shallow, but you could get lost in the maze of marshes and islands. The best way to avoid this is to use a map and follow the left shoreline going upstream. Jack Rochelle and I once got out of the channel on the right side and almost foundered. We broke a shear pin and had difficulty replacing it, because we couldn't find a place to get out of the boat without sinking to our shoe tops.

One of my favorite places to fish on the Pungo is Scranton Creek, near the community of Scranton on Highway 264. You can launch a light boat at the bridge over the creek. The landing, however, is little more than a dirt path, and the water at the landing is shallow. I have gotten stuck at the landing several times. Once I had to hitchhike to Belhaven to get a tow truck to pull my car out.

After you get your boat launched, the creek is an easy place to fish, either upstream or downstream. But the water close to the bridge is filled with grass, especially during the spring. The grass will foul both your electric motor and your outboard motor. Later in the year, after much of the grass has died, the upstream portion is better to fish in a high wind because it is more sheltered.

If you fish toward the mouth of the creek, stay well to the middle of the creek for about a quarter-mile until you pass all of the old pilings in the creek. Then you can fish either shoreline and often catch bass. There are some ponds off both sides of the creek, and they are good places to fish, too. Scranton Creek, as it nears the Pungo River, gets ever wider and can be rough in a high wind.

There are a number of other good places to fish on the Pungo and its tributaries. People who live in the area are friendly and willing to give you advice about where and how to fish for bass. But don't be surprised if you have to ask several people before finding anybody who knows much about bass fishing. Most residents ignore the sometimes fabulous freshwater fishing for the fabulous saltwater fishing that is nearby. That is fine with me. I like having miles of water to myself.

The bass in the Pungo fight harder than bass in many other places. They develop a pugnaciousness by having to compete with saltwater fish. Also, there are fewer weeds in the Pungo than in some other coastal-area waters, so the bass have more room to fight.

Bass fishing on the Pungo, especially, has been an on-again, off-again sport since I began fishing the area many years ago. I finally learned to fish for something else when I could not catch bass. Now, on most trips, I catch some kind of fish.

The best all-around bait to use for mixed-bag fishing are the lures Dave Goforth designs to be used with strips of fish or other natural bait "sweeteners." Dave's lures, however, are not widely available. The next best thing for catching a variety of fish in Pungo River country is a small jig with a natural bait sweetener fished slowly across the bottom.

A bass I remember almost as vividly as my first bass and my sons' first bass was the first one caught by my buddy and colleague, Wilt Browning. Wilt, a sportswriter for the *Greensboro News & Record*, took up fishing at 47 years of age. I took him first to lakes in Greensboro, trying to teach him what little I know about fishing. But he was not to catch a bass until he fished Pungo Creek for the first time. On that first trip to the Pungo, Wilt flipped his Tiny Torpedo to the edge of the marsh.

"Now just let it settle there before working it back to the boat," I told him.

"An explosion!" Wilt later wrote in the *News & Record*.

The bass — a big one, especially for eastern North Carolina — jumped several times.

"Don't horse him!" I kept telling Wilt.

After I slipped the landing net under the bass, Wilt said that in everything I had told him about bass fishing, I had neglected to explain what "horsing" meant.

Also on that trip were Joe Kyle, Walt Jackson, and Curtis Youngblood of Greensboro, and Harold Bebber of Elon College. That night at dinner, Harold said Wilt would remember that bass as long as he lived.

"It will cost you a thousand dollars," Walt Jackson added.

"Somehow," Wilt later wrote, "it seemed like a bargain."

The Belhaven area is a good place to stay when you fish the Pungo River. Lodging accommodations are limited, however, and you should nail down reservations as far in advance as possible.

The stately River Forest Manor at Belhaven is my favorite place to stay in all of North Carolina. It is popular with Doris Dale and wives of my fishing buddies who have stayed there. They like the elegance of the fine antique furniture and grand architecture. They also like the informal hospitality of Melba Smith and Axom Smith Jr. and their staff. The River Forest Manor's big buffet dinners are famous up and down the Inland Waterway. In the spring and fall, especially, big yachts tie up at the River Forest marina. Many well-known people have visited the River Forest Manor.

When my sons and I or other fishing buddies make stag fishing trips to the Pungo, we reserve rooms in the River Forest annex. It is not as grand (or as expensive) as the inside rooms, but it is comfortable and adequate. It is also convenient for parking our boats and charging our boat batteries. No matter where we stay, inside or outside, we always eat at least one dinner at River Forest.

If all lodging accommodations in Belhaven are booked, you can stay in little Washington, N.C., and drive the 25 miles to the Pungo. If you stay in Washington, you might want to fish one of the tributaries to the Pamlico River between Washington and Belhaven. These include such streams as Bath Creek, North Creek, and St. Clair Creek.

Bath Creek is one of the prettiest and most interesting creeks in the area. It has a good population of bass in its upper reaches. Back Creek, a tributary to Bath Creek, also is a good place to fish for bass.

Bath is a famous town. Its historic restoration program now attracts many tourists. It is also a favorite place for sailboaters, and in warm weather you even see water skiers.

You can find solitude, however, by fishing up in the creeks that run into Bath Creek and Back Creek. There is something appealing about fishing in an area that has so much history. The infamous pirate Blackbeard made his headquarters on Bath Creek. He was so elusive, people thought he traveled from one side of the creek to the other by crawling through a tunnel he had dug. In the early 1700s, he was finally killed by the British in a naval battle near the fishing village of Ocracoke on the Outer Banks. His head, swinging from a yardarm, was triumphantly brought into Bath.

There are several boat access areas in and near Bath. Fishing can also be good in creeks on the other side (the south side) of the Pamlico River. These include Blount, Durham, South, and Bond creeks.

You have still another choice about where to make your headquarters when fishing the Pungo River area. You can stay at Swan Quarter, New Holland, Fairfield, or Engelhard near Lake Mattamuskeet. Then you can fish Pungo River to the west, the Alligator River to the north, or Lake Mattamuskeet itself.

Mattamuskeet, which covers more than 30,000 acres, can be fished using the same methods you use on Currituck Sound, the Pungo, or other brackish or fresh waters in eastern North Carolina. There is one big difference, however: Mattamuskeet is even more shallow than other coastal-area bass fishing waters.

Fred Hitchcock Jr., an excellent fly-rod angler, believes that spring, as early as March, is the best season to fish the lake. Fred's favorite choice of tackle for fishing Mattamuskeet included the fly rod and a Black Widow popping bug. The bug is black with one large red spot and several gray spots. These colors are so good on Mattamuskeet that Fred painted several lures those colors for his wife to use on spinning tackle.

Most people who fish Mattamuskeet use boats. When they fish, however, they usually get out and wade, pulling their boats behind them. Mattamuskeet is deep only in the canals, and the bottom is mostly firm. You should, nevertheless, be careful when wading.

At times, you may have to fish underwater lures to catch bass on Mattamuskeet, especially in the middle of the day in mid-summer. The best choice of lures then is the Johnson spoon rigged with pork rind, rubber skirt, or the tail of an artificial worm. The artificial worm itself, rigged Texas style, can be deadly. So can spinner baits.

Much of Mattamuskeet is weedy, but in areas that are relatively free of weeds, you can catch fish on lures such as Rapalas or Rebels.

There are several public boat landings around the lake. You can stop at almost any service station, grocery store, or other business and get the latest fishing information. As in other places in eastern North Carolina, residents are neighborly and helpful.

Part 2:
Mid-State Fishing

Bass
For The
Multitudes

Chapter 10

Lakes For Urban Anglers

It has become fashionable in recent years to criticize electric companies for the destruction of our rivers and for the escalation of our electric bills. Other industries that dam rivers and the U.S. Army Corps of Engineers have also come in for a share of bad press.

These complaints may or may not be deserved. But one thing is not debatable: By creating big man-made lakes, the power companies and the Corps of Engineers have brought good bass fishing close to the doorsteps of multitudes of people.

Residents of North Carolina's largest city, Charlotte, can leave their homes and, in less than 30 minutes, launch their boats at Duke Power Company's Lake Wylie to the south or Lake Norman to the north. The residents of other large cities in the Piedmont region can find good bass fishing in reservoirs not more than an hour's drive away.

Kerr Lake, for example, draws bass anglers from all over the United States. Yet it is within easy driving distance of the state's capital, Raleigh, and a nearby city, Durham. Each year, Lake Gaston just to the east of Kerr Lake yields some of the largest bass caught in North Carolina. Lake Jordan and Falls of the Neuse Lake are even closer to Raleigh and Durham.

All these lakes offer good year-around fishing. Some anglers prefer cold weather because water skiers are in deep hibernation then. Sure, you have to be hearty to enjoy fishing Piedmont North Carolina lakes during many days in the dead of the winter. But the climate is moderate when compared to that of western North

101

Carolina (not to mention up North). Also, you can continue to catch bass when most anglers have given up on the raw and wind-swept sounds, rivers, and creeks of eastern North Carolina.

Although mid-state bass fishing is normally at its peak in the spring and fall, many good anglers say summer is best, and the water skiers be danged. These anglers claim — and back up their claims with stringers or live wells loaded with fish — that water skiers and pleasure boaters do not disturb the fish.

"Boaters bother the fisherman more than the fish," said Blake Honeycutt, one of the state's best bass anglers.

It is true that the quality of bass fishing in the large reservoirs of central North Carolina fluctuates drastically from decade to decade, and even from year to year and month to month — just as it does in eastern North Carolina and western North Carolina. Fishing on some of the lakes will be great for years, and then — within a year or two — become less than mediocre. Fortunately, this never happens to all of the lakes at the same time, and anglers willing to fish hard can still catch some bass even on the worst lakes.

High Rock Lake is a good example of how fishing changes in Piedmont lakes. In the mid-1960s, High Rock hardly rated a mention in conversations about bass fishing. But by the mid-1970s, it had improved to the point where it was one of the state's most exciting lakes for bass fishing. It is true that you couldn't catch a lot of big bass. But you could catch plenty of them.

High Rock Lake is only an hour's drive from Charlotte and even closer to such cities as Greensboro, Winston-Salem, and High Point. It is so close to Salisbury and Lexington that youngsters can pedal their bicycles to the lake and fish for bass after school lets out for the day.

The quality of bass fishing on other lakes fluctuates dramatically. Take Falls of the Neuse Lake near Raleigh, and Lake Jordan near Pittsboro. When the lakes were new in the mid-1980s, it was easy to catch a limit of bass. As they matured, however, fishing declined. After a few years of poor fishing on the lakes, things began to get better again. Chances are that fishing will never be as sensational as it once was on the lakes. But there is one bright spot: The average size of the bass you do catch should improve as the

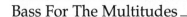
years go by.

Bass fishing on some of the Piedmont reservoirs remains consistently good year after year despite heavy fishing pressure. Lake Wylie, on the North Carolina-South Carolina border, is one of the heaviest-fished lakes in either state. Yet anglers regularly catch good numbers of fish there, and some big ones too.

Lakes in central North Carolina offer the bass angler plenty of variety, from small, shallow lakes such as Blewett Falls Lake in south-central North Carolina to huge Lake Norman, called the "Inland Sea," in the Piedmont. Or, if you prefer to fish a mountain-like lake, there is Lake Tillery in the Uwharries — mountains that once towered higher than the Rockies but have been worn down by time.

Most of these lakes give up at least one trophy bass every week in the spring, summer, and fall, and would in the winter, too, if as many people fished them then. But best of all, they are close at hand for those of us who live and work in metropolitan areas.

Catawba Chain

Chapter 11

Lake James, Hickory, Norman, Wylie, And Others

The Catawba River is born of a small, clear mountain stream in western North Carolina. As it tumbles down from the highlands, trout give way to bass — first the smallmouth, then the largemouth.

From its modest beginnings, the stream grows ever larger as it winds its way through the mountains, then the foothills, and, finally, down through the flatlands in South Carolina, where it changes its name to the Waterree.

On its way through North Carolina, it stops long enough to form a number of Duke Power Company reservoirs. First, there is Lake James near Marion and Morganton. Next comes Rhodhiss, near Valdese. Rhodhiss is followed by Lookout Lake between Statesville and Hickory. Then comes Lake Hickory at Hickory. Lake Norman, north of Charlotte, is next. The last impoundment in the North Carolina chain of Catawba lakes is Lake Wylie, which straddles the North Carolina-South Carolina state line.

Other rivers feed some of these lakes, but the Catawba is the only river common to all of them.

The Catawba lakes are, for the most part, in the center of the most populous area of North Carolina. They are also all within easy driving distance of one of the best bass fishermen in the United States: Blake Honeycutt of Hickory.

A likeable and intelligent man, Blake had been extremely successful in tournament fishing when I first met him. Yet he still fished more for fun than for money and trophies. He liked to use ultralight fishing gear when possible, simply because he felt it more sporting and challenging to catch bass that way.

Blake was still 13th on the list of all-time money winners in Bass Anglers Sportsman Society (B.A.S.S.) tournament fishing. He had won all the trophies that organization had to give between first and tenth place, with the exception of ninth. It was a remarkable record, considering he was a hard-working business owner and did not have much time to devote to tournament fishing. He had fished for bass since he was a young boy, and he first learned to use a fly rod at Lake Hickory. When he grew up, he fished all over the United States.

A conservation-minded sportsman, Blake contributed considerable time and money to the Bass Research Foundation of Starkville, Mississippi. The future of bass fishing concerned him. He thought the quality of bass fishing on the Catawba chain of lakes, with the possible exceptions of Lake Hickory and Lake Wylie, had gone downhill over the years. In the past, his success at fishing the Catawba chain had been phenomenal. He began fishing Lake Norman when it was first formed, and you could still see a glint of excitement in his eyes when he recalled those days.

"When my son was just big enough to stand up in the boat, we caught 87 bass over four pounds [each] off one point in Lake Norman. And I don't know how many we lost. That was when the lake was three years old and people said there weren't any bass in it over about a pound and a half. Man, those five- and six-pounders were everywhere. You could catch two at every bush, two at every stump."

Blake paused for breath, then added, "I'd go from the launching ramp to the first point, and sit there and catch a limit in 30 minutes, and bet you a hundred dollars I could do it day after day. And did it for three years."

But, he added gloomily, "The bass just aren't there any more, not in the quantity like they used to be. You have to work real hard for the bass you get now."

What suggestion did he have for people who don't mind working real hard for bass on the Catawba chain of lakes?

"Basically, the lakes are all different," he replied. "It's all the same water, the same river. But the lakes are at different elevations, and the seasons are slightly different."

Nevertheless, according to Blake, you can fish most parts of all the lakes using the same methods — if you consider that the seasons arrive a little earlier or later on some of the lakes.

Here is a look at the different lakes in the chain:

LAKE JAMES

Lake James covers 6,150 acres in the North Carolina foothills. "Lake James is more of a mountain lake," Blake Honeycutt pointed out. "But it is not a true mountain lake. It has a lot of bluffs on it, and the water is almost always clear. In the springtime, those bass are just about like they are anywhere else. You'll find them on the points. The lake has smallmouth bass in limited concentrations, and you can catch them off the red stumpy points and on the bluffs on the jig and eel, and the largemouth bass will also hit the jig and eel."

But Blake said he believed crankbaits were usually the best lures for largemouth in the late winter and early spring. "That's assuming we've had a normal weather pattern and the lake isn't real high and real muddy," he said.

What depth is best to fish in the late winter and early spring?

"From a foot to 20 feet deep," Blake said.

One foot? Even in February?

"Yes," Blake answered. "Then as it gets later in the spring, the fish are in the spawning process, and you can take them some on topwater, some on crankbaits, and some on plastic worms."

That continues through about the middle of June.

"Then they, of course, move out in the holes," he said. "Or what we call holes, which is basically structure off long points or submerged islands, and it's practically all worm fishing until about September. But spoons that can be used for jigging, such as the Hopkins spoon, are also good during that time of the year."

When the water begins to cool in the fall, you should switch to crankbaits again. Topwater lures are also good in the fall. In the winter, lures that can be jigged deep — lures such as the Little George and the Hopkins spoon — are once again good on Lake James.

Blake said the same general advice applies to fishing the other Catawba lakes. But he cautioned that techniques might have to be varied slightly depending on which lake you fish, and even on which part of a particular lake you fish. For example, he said fishing the Linville Gorge side of Lake James is much different than fishing the Catawba side.

"The Linville River feeds into it, and it is almost always very clear, and the fish are hard to catch," he said. "You've got to use ultralight equipment and small lures."

You can't count on catching smallmouth bass any further south than Lake James. Some anglers use spinner baits at night in the summer on the Linville side and catch many smallmouth bass in the two-to-three-pound category. In fact, the largest smallmouth bass I ever caught came from Lake James. And I caught it by accident.

Doris Dale and I went to the lake in May to get some pictures of walleyed pike I needed for a magazine story I had written. I called John Peeler of Morganton, one of the area's best fishermen, and asked for advice.

"I would use nightcrawlers," he said.

That's what we used, but John forgot to warn me that I might catch something besides walleyes.

A smallmouth took my bait in shallow water off a long point. The smallmouth immediately came up and wildly danced across the water's surface. It continued until I finally landed it with my four-pound test line and ultralight rod. I released the fish without weighing it, but there is no doubt it was the largest one I have ever caught.

I remember something else about that day, too. As Doris Dale and I fished a quiet cove between two small mountains, we heard something crashing through the underbrush. When we looked up, we saw a big buck deer plunge into the water and swim across the cove.

"Dogs must be chasing it," I said as I reached for my camera.

But before I could focus the telephoto lens, the deer splashed out of the water on the other side of the cove, shook itself off, then bounded up the hillside.

We listened for dogs, but never heard any. Meanwhile, the deer emerged from the brush on the other side of the mountain and swam across another cove. Apparently he was just taking a short-cut.

RHODHISS LAKE

At Rhodhiss Lake, said Blake Honeycutt, anglers have cut down a lot of tree laps to improve the crappie habitat. "The bass seem to hang around those trees and tree laps."

Spinner baits and crankbaits are especially effective for fishing the tree laps in the spring. The spinner bait should be worked down *into* the laps; the crankbaits should be worked just *over* the laps.

"Rhodhiss is basically like a river, long and narrow," Blake observed. In all, the lake covers 3,515 acres and has 90 miles of shoreline.

LAKE HICKORY

The next lake on the Catawba is Lake Hickory, which has 4,100 acres of water and 105 miles of shoreline. Although larger than Rhodhiss, Lake Hickory is a winding, narrow lake. Boat traffic and fishing pressure is heavy.

"But there are still many fish in the lake," said Blake.

Some of the fish in Lake Hickory are big, too.

"My wife caught an 11.75-pounder out of it," he said, confessing that her fish topped anything he had caught up to that time. "My biggest bass was 11 pounds and 2 ounces, and I caught him out of Lake Norman."

Blake said he thought Lake Hickory has more bass than any lake on the Catawba chain, with the exception of Lake Wylie. "Lake Hickory has a lot of stumpy points, rocky points, and bluffs on it," he said. "It also has a lot of good creek channels."

He said the habits of Lake Hickory bass are about like the habits of Lake James and Rhodhiss bass. "But there are more shad in Lake Hickory, so bass tend to school more on the lake than they do on most other lakes."

LOOKOUT SHOALS

Lookout Shoals is a small impoundment between Lake Hickory and Lake Norman. It has only 1,270 acres of surface and 39 miles of shoreline. If you learn to fish the other Catawba lakes, you will be able to catch bass on Lookout Shoals.

LAKE NORMAN

Lake Norman is the next lake in the Catawba chain and deserves special mention because it is the largest reservoir in North Carolina. It covers 32,510 acres and has 520 miles of shoreline. It is near Charlotte and other large cities and towns, and it has more fishing and boating traffic than any other lake in the state.

"Lake Norman is really four lakes in one," Blake Honeycutt said. "The upper four miles is more like a river."

The middle part is set in gently rolling hills. "The structure is less defined, and the water is normally more clear than the rest of the lake," Blake said.

The lower half is more flat and is usually clear, although the middle portion of the lower half can get dingy. "This is where Plant Marshall's cooling water comes in, and the water is almost always warmer than the rest of the lake."

Did Blake have any special techniques to suggest for Lake Norman?

"Well," he answered, "it boils down to a lot of hard work now. In the early spring when the lake is low and clear and fairly warm, I'd probably use crankbaits on the rocky points, and I'm sure I'd use some spinner baits back in the creeks and around the big old stumps. Sometimes, the bass will run way back in those creeks, because the creeks will warm up faster.

"Then, later on, I'd look for spawning-type areas: warm areas with gravel bottoms with some cover, and I'd use shallow-running crankbaits, worms, maybe even some spinner baits in the morning, and maybe even some topwater. Then, during post-spawning season, I'd get out in the 20- to 30-foot water on structure that had some cover on it about halfway up the creeks, if I could find any, because the fish would be starting to migrate back up the river.

"As the summer progresses, most of the fish would be off the points in the main river channel, and then I'd jig with spoons and worms. And in the fall, I'd watch for school bass. They school down there pretty good, say in December, and you can catch them on a Little George, or a crankbait, or any type of bait that you can get into them. You can even get them on topwater sometimes, and they'll hit pretty good.

"As it progressed into deep winter, I'd probably use Little Georges and Hopkins spoons exclusively."

LAKE WYLIE

The last North Carolina lake on the Catawba chain is Lake Wylie, which covers 12,455 acres and has 325 miles of shoreline. That includes the portion in South Carolina. Blake said he was not as familiar with that lake as he was with the others on the chain, so I went looking for Boyd Howard of Gastonia. I had heard that he fished Lake Wylie often and knew it well.

"I would say that Wylie would produce more fish per man-hour than any other lake in North Carolina," Boyd said. "It's heavily fished, but they still consistently take fish out of there. And big fish, too."

It was early fall when I talked to Boyd, and he had already caught two large fish on Wylie: one that weighed more than eight pounds and one that weighed more than nine. For years, Lake

Wylie has been the best lake in North Carolina for bass fishing.

Here, briefly, was Boyd's advice:

From late March to late November, fish around boathouses. Use artificial worms all year long except when the water gets so cold it inhibits the action of the plastic. During the spring and summer, try topwater baits, spinner baits, and crankbaits. In the fall, when the bass school, use Hopkins spoons. In the winter, try lures such as the Little George. And fish the spinner bait on the bottom.

Talking to Boyd brought back many fond memories. I grew up in Rock Hill, South Carolina, and began fishing Lake Wylie when I was barely big enough to hold a rod. The lake yielded some of the first bass I ever caught. Later, the first bass I caught after coming home from the Korean War was one that nailed a deep running Hawaiian Wiggler in water about six feet deep, way out from shore. That day of fishing helped make some of the worst memories of my life seem far away.

I don't think I've ever fished Lake Wylie without catching at least a few bass.

My father lived on the shores of Lake Wylie during his latter years. My sister, Mary Sue, and her family still live there. Conrad, my younger son, caught his first bass on the lake. That bass hit a Jitterbug. Conrad was so little he had to use both hands to cast his spincasting rod, and he was standing on the bank casting. I was in my sister's house and Conrad ran in yelling, "Daddy, Daddy, I caught a whopper!"

Lake Wylie has provided many other good memories. Like the early Sunday morning in the spring that my older son, John Gerard, and I fished the cove beside my sister's house. We used fly rods and had one of the most productive hours of fishing I have ever enjoyed.

A mist rose from the lake that day. Only the birds chirping broke the stillness. Within an hour, I caught my limit. John, who was just learning to use a fly rod, lost several fish. Then a big speedboat, operated by someone who must have been trying to shake off the dregs of a bad Saturday night, cut into the cove. Upon seeing us, he gunned his motor and left our small boat awash in his wake. The bass quit hitting on top.

My father used an unusual, but productive, technique for fishing Lake Wylie. He tightened the steering mechanism on his outboard motor so the boat would run straight even if left to guide itself. Then he ran from one spot to another, spots he had found to be productive during the many years he had fished the lake. Upon approaching a favorite spot, he would shift the motor into neutral and make several casts with an underwater lure that could be worked fast, like a Cordell Hot Spot. Then he would run to another of his favorite spots and make several casts. He never cut off the motor.

Using this method, Dad often caught his limit in an hour or two of fishing. He usually fished piers, stumps, boathouses, and rocky points.

Once when I fished with him, the boathouse he was fishing creaked from the wake of his skiff.

"You would think that noise would scare the fish," I said.

"Son, those fish hear that noise a hundred times a day with all the boats running up and down this lake," he answered in the same patient tone he had used when I was a small boy many years earlier. "So the bass get used to it." As if to emphasize his point, Dad pulled a small boat out from under the boathouse a few casts later.

Dad and his brother, Ralph, and their fishing friends used the same method on other lakes, and they caught more bass than most other anglers. Dad never admitted it, but I think he developed the fast-fishing technique after he suffered a heart attack.

Dad often fished Lake Wylie a few hours during the late afternoons after he drove home from about ten miles away. He also fished all day most Wednesdays. He and his friends enjoyed taking a break at noon and cooking lunch. They just about always caught enough bass to eat.

Dad had a technique for fishing artificial worms on Lake Wylie that was similar to one Boyd Howard used. In the late winter and early spring, Dad fished what he called "a little green worm." The worm was actually a Fish Finder made in Gastonia. The worm has two small hooks made of light wire that bend if you put enough pressure on them. The hooks are not weedless.

Dad rigged a slip sinker on his line above a swivel. Then he tied about 14 inches of line below the swivel and attached the worm to the end of that. Because the worm was below the sinker, it didn't get hung up as often as it would have if it had been against the worm.

Dad used heavy line, and he would cast or drop the worm into brush piles. If the worm snagged, Dad wrenched it free. Then he used pliers to bend the hooks back into their original shape. He fished the worm very slowly, occasionally pumping his rod. He caught a lot of fish that way and lost far fewer than I do when I use the "Texas rig." I think his success was due to the fact that the hook didn't have to first penetrate the worm as it does if rigged Texas-style.

Years after Dad taught me this method, Blake Honeycutt described a similar rig to me. He called it the "South Carolina rig."

But other lures are effective, too. Mike Rainey, a nephew who lives on Lake Wylie, caught 35 bass in an hour and a half while casting a Hellbender. He cast it off a point in the lake and reeled in fast so the lure ran deep. When he stopped fishing that day, he weighed the smallest and largest fish he had caught. The smallest weighed 5.75 pounds. The largest weighed almost 11 pounds.

It was a short day of fishing, too. It was June, and it rained the entire time Mike was fishing. Thunder and lightning finally ran him off the lake.

GENERAL INFORMATION

Duke Power Company has some excellent public recreation areas around the Catawba lakes. The utility company also has free launching sites on the lakes. There are many other free or commercial ramps on the lakes as well. Free maps that list the ramps,

marinas, picnic areas, boat rentals, and other information may be
obtained by writing:

Duke Power Company
Public Relations Department
P.O. Box 2178
Charlotte, N.C. 28201

You'll have little trouble finding lodging in these areas. Good
restaurants and campgrounds are plentiful.

One final word of caution about fishing Lake Wylie, however:
North Carolina and South Carolina don't have reciprocal fishing
license agreements. If you want to fish the South Carolina portion
of the lake, you must have a South Carolina non-resident license. If
you have only a North Carolina license, be sure you don't stray
over into South Carolina. South Carolina game protectors know
where the state line is, even if the bass don't.

Yadkin And Pee Dee Reservoirs

Chapter 12

Or, Apologies To A Friend

Jack Bilyeu reeled in about the 40th largemouth bass we had caught. It reminded me once again that I should apologize to George "Speedy" Lohr of Southmont, N.C., and to my friend, Bill Hicks. Here is why:

Bill lived at High Rock Lake in the Piedmont region of North Carolina, the first lake in the chain of Yadkin River impoundments. Over the years, I had come to know Bill because he was a member of a loose-knit club to which I belonged. The sole purpose of the club was to make two fishing trips to northeastern North Carolina's Currituck Sound each year, one in the spring and one in the fall. So when I started to look for an expert to tell me how to catch fish on the Yadkin River lakes, I turned to Bill for help. Bill suggested I get in touch with Speedy Lohr, the owner of Speedy's Place — a combination restaurant, tackle shop, and grocery store near High Rock Lake.

"Sure," Speedy said when I called. "I'll be glad to talk to you. Why don't you come down tomorrow?"

I drove to Southmont the next morning and interrupted Speedy, who was washing his bass boat in front of his store. He said he fished mostly on his home lakes of High Rock, Tuckertown, and Badin. Then, after making a final swipe at his boat, he invited me into his restaurant and ordered us cups of coffee. Although it was a steamy July day, the coffee tasted good.

Between sips, Speedy fired answers to my questions. In the process, he made the following claims for bass fishing on High Rock Lake:

117

— "High Rock is easy to fish. We've got the stumps and marshes. I mean it's easy for a stranger to fish."

— "High Rock is as good a lake as there is in the state...it's nothing for you to catch your limit...two or three times a day."

— "There are so many fish in High Rock, if you go out there and keep moving, you'll find them."

— "In the summertime, if you get into them, you might catch your limit just *Bam! Bam! Bam!*"

— "Just an average weekend fisherman can catch a limit of bass out of High Rock." He did qualify that statement by saying that although it is easy to catch a lot of bass in High Rock, it is not easy to catch big bass. "Most of the bass are small."

After that lone disclaimer, he went on to assert, "You can catch bass in shallow water all year long on High Rock, Tucker-town, and Badin."

That was too much. "Even now?" I asked skeptically. "Even now, you catch bass in shallow water?" Looking through the window, I could see heat waves dancing on the pavement of Highway 8 in front of Speedy's Place.

"Even now," Speedy shot back. "The water gets hot. But the fish stay shallow for some reason. I think it might have something to do with oxygen." He sensed my disbelief and elaborated, "I'd say 98 percent of the fishermen never throw a lure any deeper than in 15 feet of water."

Speedy asked the waitress to bring us fresh cups of coffee, then continued. "We had a tournament Saturday, and I bet there was not a bass caught deeper than ten feet."

He declared that bass fishing in High Rock was much better now than when he had started fishing the lake more than 30 years earlier. The fishing had improved greatly just in the past few years, he said.

As I listened to Speedy that hot July day, I remembered my experience fishing on High Rock. The last time I had fished the lake was about seven years earlier. The fishing had been so bad I decided never to fish it again, no matter how convenient it was to my home in Greensboro. I turned my attention to other lakes farther from home: Lake Norman (at that time a hot bass lake), Kerr Lake, Lake Gaston, the Alligator River, Currituck Sound, and other exotic places, including some Florida water. It is true in fishing, as in other things, that distance lends enchantment.

So who could blame me, knowing the poor fishing I had experienced on High Rock, for reacting dubiously as I listened to Speedy's glowing report? Not that I had any reason to doubt Speedy's veracity; I didn't know him well enough for that.

Still, he did run a business near High Rock Lake, a business that depended at least partly on anglers. I reasoned that it would be understandable if he used a business person's license in describing the quality of fishing on the lake.

So the next time I saw Jack Bilyeu, one of my fishing buddies, I told him what Speedy had said. And I told him I had doubts. "There's only one way to settle the burning issue," I said. We should conduct a scientific test: We should fish the lake. Jack said he guessed he would be willing to go fishing — if I were sure it was for the sake of science.

Exactly five days after I first talked to Speedy, Jack and I hooked my boat to my car in the pre-dawn darkness. Then we headed for High Rock Lake. With time out for breakfast at Bill's Truck Stop in Lexington, we arrived at a boat landing near the mouth of Swearing Creek just as the sun was peeping up over the high corn near the lake. (Swearing Creek is a tributary to High Rock.)

It was still early morning, but the July heat was already oppressive. Even so, a few hours later, I made a promise: If I ever visited Speedy Lohr on another hot July day, and if he predicted snow, I would look for my overcoat. And put it on.

Jack and I caught so many largemouth bass that we quit counting after releasing 26 before noon. The temperature hovered around 95 degrees Fahrenheit and the water was tepid to the touch, yet Jack and I caught all of our bass in shallow water. Most hit right at the bank, where my depth finder recorded less than three feet of water, and the boat was only a cast away from shore. I figured the depth of the water where we caught most of the bass was about a foot, because my lure struck bottom almost as soon as it hit the water.

Jack and I tried fishing deeper water in High Rock Lake. Some of the water was what the bass "professionals" would have described as perfect places for fish in hot weather. We didn't get a bump. As soon as we returned to shallow water, it was just like Speedy guaranteed: *Bam! Bam! Bam!*

We caught some fish in such shallow water that I thought my depth finder must have gone wacky. When I stuck a paddle in the water, however, it confirmed the readings of the finder. I recalled my doubts when Speedy had said, "The water gets hot. But the bass stay shallow."

My conscience again pained me for doubting Speedy.

The bass were fun to catch. But they were small. I remembered Speedy cautioning that, although you could catch a lot of bass in High Rock Lake, you wouldn't catch many big ones. That made him right on Count Number 2 of his claims for High Rock Lake fishing.

The places we fished were filled with rocks, snags, stumps, fallen trees, overhanging bushes, and all of the other things that make a bass fishing lake productive. "High Rock is easy to fish" — that's what Speedy Lohr had said five days earlier — "I mean it's easy for a stranger to fish." That made him right on Count Number 3.

As Jack reeled in still another small bass, I couldn't believe I had been skeptical when Speedy looked me straight in the eye and declared, "It's nothing to catch your limit two or three times a day." Jack and I had already caught and released our limits and it was still early. That made Speedy right on Count Number 4. I realized he was right about everything he had told me.

At the time, I was an unskilled artificial worm fisherman. Yet I caught all my bass on a worm. I used an eight-ounce slip sinker and crawled the worm across the bottom. Most of the time, the bass hit with such force they hooked themselves. Some grabbed the worm as soon as it hit the water.

Jack and I caught so many largemouth that when we saw white bass schooling on top, we put down our bass rods and started fishing for white bass with our ultralight rods. We must have caught 50 or 60 white bass.

When we grew tired of that, we switched back to our artificial worms and starting catching largemouth again. When measured by the number of largemouth bass we landed, that was the best day of fishing I ever had while using an artificial worm. I had caught larger bass on a worm, but never as many.

I decided that George "Speedy" Lohr was the most honest man I had ever met. Bill Hicks had told me that Speedy was an authority on High Rock Lake bass fishing, as well as fishing on Tuckertown and Badin lakes. Speedy admitted he didn't know as much about fishing on Lake Tillery. (The Yadkin River changes its name to the Pee Dee River just before it flows into Lake Tillery.)

Speedy's favorite method of fishing High Rock, Tuckertown, and Badin was with deep-running crankbaits. He used them all year long, switching to other baits only occasionally.

"We use the Bagley B's, or about any crank-down plugs, such as the deep-running Rebel or something like that, and we fish the shallow water," he said.

Fishing deep-running lures all year long in shallow water seemed highly unorthodox when Speedy first mentioned it. The more I thought about it, however, the more it made sense — especially on the Yadkin River lakes. He was giving the fish an opportunity to hit in both shallow and moderately deep water.

Speedy said he stationed his boat within casting distance of the shoreline and slowly moved parallel to the shore, casting toward the bank with his crankbaits. As soon as the lure hit the water, he cranked it down to the bottom. He kept it on the bottom all through the retrieve. That way, the lure explored all depths between the bank and the boat. Speedy used the same method in the fall, winter, spring, and summer. He used the crankbaits in shallow water, even in the middle of the summer. Only occasionally would he switch to something else.

"I don't change much," he said. "Except I do go to the worm sometimes when it gets real hot."

When he did grudgingly switch to the worm, he used a light slip sinker and a small worm.

"I like the seven-and-a-half-inch worm in the main," he explained.

He used the "Texas rig" and had caught fish on all colors of worms.

Although Speedy fished the deep-running crankbaits most of the time, some experienced anglers have good luck using shallow-running lures. The perfect time for shallow-running lures is when the lakes are full and the water is up in the bushes in the fall and spring. Rapalas, Rebels, and similar lures are the choice of many anglers then. Topwater lures are also good under the same conditions. "But they are not too popular," Speedy said.

A fly rod can be effective if conditions are just right, but not many people use fly rods on the Yadkin lakes. "It can be a lot of sport, though, when they're hitting," Speedy said.

Speedy mentioned that he sometimes used another type of lure: one that resembled shad when the bass were feeding on that bait fish. His favorite lures for those times included the Bomber Speed Shad and the Cordell Hot Spot.

In addition to fishing shallow water, Speedy also fished piers in hot weather. "We've got a lot of piers, and you can catch fish under them in hot weather," he said.

Speedy pointed out that he varied the way he fished his crankbaits in the fall. "The [water level in the] lake is usually down. You just hit the little rocky points, and the ledges, and you fish close to deeper water. That's really our best fishing in the fall, as far as I'm concerned."

According to Speedy, December and January are normally the worst months for bass fishing on High Rock and the other Yadkin lakes, and spring is the best time.

Speedy said he fished Tuckertown and Badin lakes about the same way he fished High Rock — with a few exceptions. He didn't think there were as many bass on Tuckertown as on High Rock, but added, "For a man looking for big bass, Tuckertown is a good lake."

Tuckertown is between High Rock and Badin and is a smaller lake. It is shallow and has a lot of stumps.

"The crankbaits are good there, too," Speedy said, "and I'd

fish it about like I'd fish High Rock, except I'd go to a spinner bait a whole lot more down there. I don't use spinner baits much on High Rock."

He said he fished the spinner bait almost exclusively on Tuckertown in the spring. He buzzed it when fish were getting ready to spawn, but fished it under water during other times of the year.

In the summer, he fished the worm along with crankbaits. The rest of the year, he followed the same pattern he used on High Rock.

The same general methods that work on High Rock work on Badin Lake — with one big difference. "Badin usually stays crystal clear, so I use smaller lures and smaller line and use even smaller worms," Speedy said.

There are a number of commercial and state-operated boat ramps on the Yadkin River lakes. High Rock, Tuckertown, and Badin lakes are all within 50 miles of both Greensboro and Winston-Salem, and even closer to Lexington, Salisbury, Thomasville, and High Point. Interstate 85 passes very close to High Rock Lake, which is the northernmost of the three.

By the way, a couple of years after I first met Speedy Lohr, I lost touch with Bill Hicks, the man who told me that Speedy was an authority on fishing the Yadkin lakes. Later, I heard that Bill had entered the ministry. I was not surprised.

LAKE TILLERY

Lake Tillery in the Uwharrie Mountains is one of the prettiest lakes in North Carolina. The water is almost always clear. There is still a lot of unspoiled countryside around Tillery despite the lake's close proximity to some of the state's largest cities. People still hunt for deer in the Uwharries.

Albemarle, Ben Morris's town, is only a few miles from Lake Tillery. One of the first things Ben told me when I first met him was that he lived on the right side of town. The right side, in his mind, however, had nothing to do with wealth or social standing. It is the nearest side of the town to Lake Tillery.

Most of the year, Ben could enjoy a couple of hours of after-noon fishing after leaving his job as city clerk and treasurer for the town of Albemarle. "From my house, I can be on the lake in about ten minutes," he explained. "I fish Tillery on the average of several times a week."

Ben had fished the lake regularly since about 1943, and he had the reputation of being one of the best bass anglers in the area. He fished the lake all year, but thought late winter and early spring were the best times for catching bass.

Ben's son, Charles, who was then a teenager, once caught an eight-pound bass while fishing Tillery on Christmas Eve. "He caught him on a Hot-N-Tot," said Ben, his voice full of fatherly pride. "He was fishing on a shallow, grassy point."

In that respect, Lake Tillery is like other lakes on the Yadkin-Pee Dee chain. You can catch bass in shallow water year-round. "I do not usually fish more than ten feet deep," Ben said.

The artificial worm is usually effective on Tillery in the spring and fall. Ben had a twist to the way he fished the artificial worm: he twisted the head to give it more action. Most of the time, he rigged the worm "South Carolina style," or about ten inches below a slip sinker. This allows the worm to ride just off the bottom.

Topwater lures are also good in the spring and fall. Ben's choice of topwater lures included the Rapalas, Bang-O-Lures, and others of that type. "Instead of swimming the lures through the water, I pop it right across the surface. It's deadly."

Ben liked to use the Heddon's Tiny Chugger topwater lure, too. In the fall, he used a special kind of crankbait. "Normally, it's a homemade lure," he explained. "The boys in the Troy B.A.S.S. club make some of their own lures. They are very good."

The lures are made of balsa, oak, cedar, or soft pine, and they are "fat" lures.

Ben used about the same tactics in the fall that he used in the spring. But in the fall, fish are usually in deeper water than they are in the spring. Also, they don't bunch up as much.

According to Ben, the worm and the Bill Norman Little

Scooper are good lures to use in the late spring and early summer, when the water begins to warm. "Usually, we fish it about a medium speed," he said of the Little Scooper. "Normally, you can catch your limit of small bass with it."

On really hot days in the summer, the worm is usually the best lure to use on Lake Tillery. A topwater lure can also be good in the summer when it is rainy or overcast.

"Sometimes, in the summer, we'll go down rock banks and cast parallel to the bank as best we can, using alphabet lures or other plugs, depending on how deep the fish are."

In midwinter, fishing is often erratic on Tillery. That's about the only time of the year when the artificial worm is ineffective on the lake. The lower temperatures inhibit the action of the plastic. "During the winter, you just about have to experiment," Ben said. One of the best bets for winter fishing on Lake Tillery, he re- marked, is a small lure fished very slowly.

Just as on the other three Yadkin and Pee Dee lakes, January is usually the worst month for fishing Tillery. There are exceptions, however. "The best string of fish I ever saw come out of Tillery was on New Year's day," Ben recalled. "A man had eight bass that weighed close to [a total of] 60 pounds. He caught them schooling and got them on plugs." That January had been warmer than normal.

As on most lakes near metropolitan areas, it is better to fish Tillery on weekdays. Summer weekends bring out hordes of water skiers. Most of the time, however, you can still find some relatively quiet water by running up into a cove or a creek.

The N.C. Wildlife Resources Commission operates four boat landings on the lake. There are also several other landings scattered around Tillery. Ben recommended putting your boat in at the landing near the bridge where Highway 24-27 crosses the Pee Dee River. "From there, you can go down the lake or up the river. My best fishing has generally been in the area of that bridge."

One reason this area is good is that it has many different kinds of water. "There's deep water," Ben said. "There's shallow water. There's grass. There are a few stumps. There's a creek that's very good. There are coves...."

Perhaps the most unusual bass cover in that area is an old bridge abutment that runs across the river south of the Highway 24-27 bridge. The U.S. Army at one time used the bridge for artillery practice, but failed to destroy the abutment. The army also left chunks of concrete in the water. Bass fishing around the debris is good.

Ben noted that a person doesn't need a fancy bass boat to fish Tillery. "A good stable 14-foot boat is ideal for this lake."

But it's helpful to bring along a depth finder and a simple temperature gauge.

BLEWETT FALLS

Blewett Falls is the last reservoir on the North Carolina portion of the Pee Dee River. It has a personality all its own.

It is shallow and can be dangerous for the hot-rod boater. The water level can fluctuate rapidly, and there are a lot of stumps. But these hindrances are a blessing to the bass angler who is more interested in fishing than in racing up and down a lake at high speeds.

Blewett Falls has the reputation for being one of the best lakes in the state for spring and fall topwater fishing. The spinner bait is especially popular, because it's deadly when fished around the stumps and logs. Depending on the time of year and the mood of the bass, the spinner bait is buzzed on top, fished just below the surface, or bumped along the bottom.

Most years, fall is the best season to fish Blewett. Although spring fishing can be good, the lake is more often muddy in the spring than in the fall. Otherwise, you can fish Blewett about like Ben Morris and Speedy Lohr fish the other lakes on the Yadkin and Pee Dee rivers.

Blewett Falls is between Rockingham and Wadesboro. You can launch your boat at two N.C. Wildlife Resources Commission ramps or one of several commercial ramps.

The only other lake in the chain, Falls (not to be confused with the lake in Wake and Durham counties that has a similar name), is so small it escapes the attention of most bass anglers. It's just a little more than a mile in length and isn't famous for large numbers of bass. The chances of catching a big bass, however, are better than average. This lake is in Stanly County near the town of Badin.

Kerr, Gaston, And Others

Chapter 13

Some Of The Best In The Country?

Although there was a light chop on Kerr Lake when the sun came up that morning in early March, there was little to warn anglers of what was to come. But by 11 a.m., winds had reached gale force, and waves spawned whitecaps in unsheltered areas of the lake. Trees bent. Limbs broke off, crashing into the water.

That night, fires flickered on all sides of the main body of the lake. The fires were built by anglers who had pulled their boats ashore, wisely deciding to spend the night in uncomfortable surroundings rather than risk the trip back across the open water.

Bill Black and I were scheduled to meet Howard Carr and Clark White at noon at a picnic shelter on one of the protected arms of the lake. We had planned to cook our lunches. But Bill and I were in my 14-foot aluminum skiff, and the high winds forced us to pick our way slowly across the water.

Howard, an insurance man, and Clark, a stockbroker, were fishing in Clark's boat. Clark's boat was larger than the average bass boat and could handle rough water. Besides, Clark and Howard were in a sheltered part of the lake. Still, the water was rough enough to be bothersome. Clark and Howard later recalled what happened.

Howard, a retired naval officer, told Clark he wasn't worried when Bill and I failed to arrive at the appointed time. Not yet. "Let's go fish that point," Clark said, pointing to the arm of the lake across from the picnic table. "Then, if they haven't shown up, we'll go look for them."

Clark moved his boat to the point, and he and Howard began

casting. At about the same time, the last angler who had used the launching ramp at the picnic area that morning decided he had fought the wind long enough. He pulled his boat out of the water and drove away. Now the only sign of human life was Howard and Clark.

This was the first time Clark had ever fished Kerr Lake. He owned a place at Lake Norman, about 200 miles southwest, and had fished that lake regularly for the past two years. Despite that, he had never caught a bragging-size largemouth bass. He had promised himself that if he ever caught a bass that weighed over eight pounds, he would have it mounted.

Now, however, Clark was not optimistic about his chances of catching a large bass. He was thinking that he had chosen a less-than-ideal day for his first fishing trip to the nationally famous lake. But as sometimes happens....

"We just decided to make a few more casts while waiting for you," Clark told Bill and me when we finally arrived about 45 minutes late. Then, modestly — at least he tried to appear modest — Clark hefted his stringer from the water. On the end was a large-mouth bass that later tipped calibrated scales at better than 8.5 pounds. And that was 24 hours after Clark had caught the bass. As anybody who fishes know, bass usually lose some of their weight after they're out of the water for awhile.

The big bass fell victim to an artificial worm that Clark had bumped slowly across the bottom of the lake.

Many of the most famous anglers in the United States rank Kerr Lake as one of the nation's best lakes for bass fishing. For years, the lake consistently showed up as one of the best ten in votes by tournament anglers and in surveys conducted by national fishing magazines. The lake is in north-central North Carolina. It lies partly in Virginia, where many people know it as Buggs Island, and partly in North Carolina.

Early on the morning that Clark caught his big bass, we had stopped by to see Jimmy Harrell to ask his advice about fishing Kerr Lake. Jimmy, a fine bass angler, learned the lake well during the years he operated a grocery store and tackle shop on the lake and did some guiding. During those years, he also became an authority on the fishing at Lake Gaston, just a few miles east of Kerr Lake. Jimmy agreed with the anglers who voted Kerr Lake one of the best bass producers in the country.

"But," he added, "fishing is beginning to show the effects of all the pressure on the lake. Five to six years ago, you could go up there and catch your limit two or three times a day. Now, due to the publicity that B.A.S.S. [Bass Anglers Sportsman Society] has given it, there has been more and more pressure on it. And the fish are beginning to be harder to find."

Jimmy told us, however, that we were fishing the lake during one of the best times. "The best time to go to Kerr Lake is any time from March through June for bank fishing, and from September through December, also for bank fishing."

By "bank fishing," Jimmy meant fishing the shoreline from a boat, not fishing from the bank of the lake.

Good spring fishing arrives a few weeks earlier on Lake Gaston than it does on Kerr Lake. So does good fall fishing. "Gaston is real good in February, from around the end of February on up through June," Jimmy said.

What lures would Jimmy recommend during those times?

"Well, in the first part of the spring, the best lures are your running plugs, such as Hellbenders, Water Dogs, and about any other deep-diving plugs. As time goes on and the bass begin moving up into the willow bushes, use your spinner baits and buzz them across the bushes."

How about topwater lures?

"They are real good, too, especially around June when the bass are through spawning," Jimmy said. "The bass are real active then and will hit about anything that moves around the bushes."

Topwater arrives at Gaston a little earlier, usually in May.

Jimmy explained that Kerr, as such a big lake, warms more slowly than most other lakes. It also is fed by a number of creeks in addition to the rivers. These help keep the lake cool.

When asked to suggest the best topwater lures for Kerr and Gaston, Jimmy answered, "I find the Devils Horse is just about the best you can use." He also liked the Bang-O-Lure. "It's kind of a topwater lure. Or you can use it so it will kind of dart down beside the willows. It is good that way, sometimes. As soon as you come to a willow tree, stop it and let it rise right beside the tree. Then dart it back down again. A lot of times, they will hit it right then."

Rebels and Rapalas are similar to the Bang-O-Lure and can be fished about the same way.

Jimmy had some advice about fishing that goes against what many anglers assume: Fish out from the banks, even in the spring, if the water is clear. "If the water is real clear, the bass aren't going to be up there on the bank. If it's kind of dingy or dark, then you're going to find your bass lying on the banks."

As the year moved into summer on Kerr and Gaston, Jimmy changed to the Little George lure, the Hopkins spoon, and the artificial worm. "Then you need to go to your deep drops, your creek channels, submerged islands with such things as stumps, rocks, underwater trees, and other stuff like that," Jimmy said. "The deeper the water is, the cooler it is."

He said the best way to fish deep water in the summer is to station your boat in shallow water and cast to the drops.

Jimmy agreed with Blake Honeycutt, the well-known Hickory bass fisherman, that summer is one of the best times of the year to catch a lot of fish. "Once you find them," Blake once told me, "they are more bunched up. I like to fish in the middle of the day, even in the hot summer."

Jimmy Harrell said that when the water on Kerr Lake began to cool in the fall, he switched back to the same type of fishing that he used in the spring. "From about the middle of October into November, you should start plugging the banks again."

When the water cools back to around 70 degrees Fahrenheit, topwater baits once again become good on both Kerr and Gaston. Again, remember that fall topwater fishing arrives a little later on Kerr than it does on Gaston because the water cools a little more slowly.

I've had some good fly-rod fishing on Kerr Lake in the fall. Neighbor Bill Jerome and I once fished the lake together in October with good results. But at first we didn't have much luck. We put the boat in at Nutbush Creek and fished half a day without getting a strike. I fished my fly rod and baitcasting rod, and Bill fished his spinning rod. I had been working on the first edition of this book for about three months at that time.

"I tell you something," I told Bill. "I think I am going to burn my book manuscript when I get home. Anybody who can't catch a bass doesn't have any business writing about fishing."

Bill thought I was serious. "You don't want to do that," he said. Several more times that morning, he urged me not to burn the manuscript.

At noon, we pulled up to the bank for lunch. Bill got out and tied the rope to a tree. I made one last cast with my Bomber before getting out of the boat. A five-pound bass nailed the lure.

"Well," I said, "I guess I won't have to burn the book after all."

"Whew," said Bill.

After lunch, Bill began catching bass on his spinning rod, and I got a strike on my fly rod just about every time I cast to a stump or stick-up. For some reason, I've never caught a bass on a fly rod in Kerr Lake in the spring, even though I've tried many times.

Jimmy Harrell told me he fished Kerr Lake in the winter about the same way he fished it the summer. But in cold weather, he said, he anchored his boat in deep water and cast toward shallow water — just the opposite of what he did in the summer.

The best lures to use in the winter on Kerr Lake are lures you can jig, such as the Little George and the Hopkins spoon.

Jimmy believed fishing is best at Kerr Lake when the water is high. "When the water has been rising and has quit rising, it doesn't make any difference whether it's hot or cold," he said. "The bass are going to be up in the bushes. There are thousands and thousands of willow trees in the water. The best thing is to hit your bushes and points with bushes."

On the other hand, he said he didn't have much luck when the water level was still dropping. "That messes the lake up. It is all right after it quits falling. In fact, that's the only time, when the water is down, when you need to fish the creek channels and the drops. Anytime the water is falling for about two or three days, it seems to affect the fishing real bad."

Jimmy ticked off his favorite places to fish. "In the spring, from about March on, I think the best place to fish is down around the Satterwhite end, because there are a whole lot more willow trees down there. As the summer progresses, I move back up into Panhandle and Grassy Creek and Island Creek, because those areas have a lot more drops and creek channels."

It is true that Gaston and Kerr can be fished using about the same methods. But the lakes have different characteristics. Among other things, Gaston is more developed. There are many houses and cottages on the lake, so there is more boat traffic.

"Gaston is a good place to fish during the week," Jimmy observed. "But it gets crowded on the weekends."

Jimmy, however, agreed with Blake Honeycutt that boaters and skiers seem to bother anglers more than the fish. "I've done pretty well at Gaston, even when the water was filled with skiers," said Jimmy. "I won a tournament up there when there were water skiers all around."

There is another reason why an angler can find more solitude at Kerr than at Gaston: Kerr is much larger. "There's about 800 miles of shoreline and most of it is undeveloped," Jimmy pointed out.

Even when there are lots of boats on Kerr, anglers can usually find places to get away from the crowds. "There are many little creeks and other places you can hide in," Jimmy said.

He described Gaston as a "clean" lake when compared with Kerr. He was not talking about litter or water pollution, but rather about such things as trees that fall into the water. "When a tree falls in the water at Gaston, they cut it out."

Would Jimmy name his favorite places to fish on Gaston?

"I like to fish down around Pea Hill, Jimmy's Creek, and Lizard Creek," he said. (Jimmy's Creek isn't named for Jimmy Harrell, though it's appropriate.)

When Jimmy first started fishing the two lakes he used ultralight equipment, but switched to baitcasting gear and 20-pound test line after losing a lot of lures. "There are a lot of obstructions you have to pull through, especially on Kerr."

After switching to baitcasting gear, he continued using spinning gear only when casting worms with light weights. He preferred to use plugs, but would tie on a worm when he felt that was the best lure to use.

Jimmy said that if he were fishing Kerr Lake or Lake Gaston for the first time, he would stop at one of the many small stores that sell groceries and fishing tackle. Most have maps of the lake. "Then I'd ask the store owners to show me where the best landings are and where the best fishing is."

You can also learn a lot about the lakes by obtaining copies of the *Bass Structure Fishing Atlas* for the two lakes. The publisher is:

Alexandria Drafting Co.
417 Clifford Avenue
Alexandria, Virginia 22035

To fish the North Carolina portion of Kerr Lake, Henderson and Oxford are convenient places to stay. Both are within short drives of the lake. In case you don't catch fish at Kerr Lake, keep in mind that Henderson is a little closer to Lake Gaston than is Oxford.

Satterwhite Point, Nutbush Creek, and several other good places to launch your boat are only about a 15-minute drive from Henderson. One reason I like to fish those places is that they are almost always clear, even when much of the rest of the lake is muddy.

Another popular place to stay is Clarksville, Virginia. North Carolina and Virginia have reciprocal fishing license agreements for lakes whose waters spread across the state line. A North Carolina fishing license will permit you to fish the Virginia portions of Kerr Lake and Lake Gaston, and vice versa.

Four rivers feed Kerr Lake: the Roanoke, Dan, Hyco, and Bannister. The Hyco also feeds Hyco Reservoir, a small lake near Roxboro. Hyco Reservoir was one of the state's hottest bass lakes when it was first opened. But as the lake got older, the quality of its bass fishing declined.

To the east of Lake Gaston, so near it is almost part of that lake, is Roanoke Rapids Lake. You can fish both Hyco and Roanoke Rapids Lake about the same way you fish Kerr and Gaston.

One last word about Kerr and Gaston: both have good populations of striped bass. Kerr is one of the few freshwater lakes in the country where stripers reproduce. The stripers in Gaston, on the other hand, are "put and take" fish — they are stocked in the lake and live out their lives without reproducing.

People who fish exclusively for striped bass on Kerr and Gaston usually employ techniques that are different than those used by people who fish exclusively for largemouth bass. Still, you sometimes catch big striped bass while fishing for largemouth bass, so don't be surprised if you hook a striper that weighs 15 or 20 pounds while you're fishing for largemouth.

Once, while fishing Kerr Lake with my younger son, Conrad, I caught a striper that weighed better than 15 pounds. When I finally landed it after a battle that took about five minutes, Conrad said, "Look how far our boat has moved."

The feisty striper had towed my aluminum skiff about an eighth of a mile.

You Expected
A Strike
Every Cast

Chapter 14

Topwater Action In December

"We'll go anywhere you want to go," Woody Tilley said over the telephone.

Woody, a Greensboro lawyer and a good friend, knew how much I was looking forward to the next day. It was to be my first out-of-town fishing trip since my heart attack six months earlier.

"But why don't we go to Lake Jordan?" Woody added. "A friend says the bass are tearing it up there."

Woody's enthusiasm crackled over the phone line. So I changed my mind about proposing a trip to Kerr Lake on the North Carolina-Virginia state line to fish for striped bass. But then Woody said something that gave me second thoughts.

"I'm not trying to tell you what to do," he said. "But why don't you bring your fly rod?"

I looked at my calendar. I thought I probably should stay home and do some shopping instead of going fishing. It was the second week in December.

"My friend says they were hitting on top," Woody said.

Woody's friend must be pulling Woody's leg, I mused as I decided to leave my fly rod at home. After all, Woody and I were not going to Florida. We were planning a day trip to a lake only about 50 miles from our Greensboro homes. I had never caught a bass on top of the water so near home in December, and I never used anything on my fly rod except a floating bug. Still, I thought it would be interesting to try a lake I had never fished. Lake Jordan — named after B. Everette Jordan, the late U.S. senator — was new at that time.

"Well," I said, "let's try Jordan, then."

The next morning, Woody and I stopped for a leisurely break-fast at the Holiday Inn in Burlington, and then drove to Pittsboro and put our boat in the water at a public landing on Lake Jordan. Woody tied a spinner bait on the end of his line, and I used a diving lure. We started fishing right at the boat landing. About 15 minutes later, we still had not felt a tap. Woody changed to a Dalton's Special, a topwater lure that has a slanted face and, on its rear, a propeller. He cast the lure out among some flooded willows whose tops were sticking out of the water.

Woody's friend would really be laughing if he could see Woody now, I thought. Woody, a very good angler, was now the fish; he had swallowed his friend's bait. I watched as Woody retrieved the Dalton's Special in spurts. The plug trailed a string of iridescent bubbles on the clear water — for about four feet. Then, *Whooosh!*

A bass rolled at it.

Woody did something I didn't see him do very often. He missed the fish.

But before I could rummage through my tackle box and, with trembling fingers, extract a topwater lure and tie on my line, I heard another *Whoosh!* Woody landed a small bass. I didn't have a Dalton's Special, but I figured a Tiny Torpedo had a similar action. I found one at last and caught a small bass on my fourth cast.

That began a day of some of the most sensational bass fishing I've ever experienced. Woody and I caught more than 100 bass.

We caught bass in the willows. We caught bass on shallow, sandy banks. We caught bass on top of the water. We caught bass in shallow water. We caught bass bumping along the bottom in deep water. We caught bass on riprap around bridges. We caught bass in snaggy water. We caught bass in open water.

We caught bass on artificial worms, topwater lures, deep-running lures, shallow-running lures, large lures, and small lures. We caught bass casting. We caught bass jigging.

As Woody later recalled, "I remember that we experimented to see if we could find a lure that the bass *wouldn't* hit."

We couldn't. Once, when I looked to see what lure Woody was

using that moment, he was casting a saltwater lure. He caught freshwater bass on it.

It was one of the few times in more than 50 years of fishing that I grew weary of catching bass. I substituted a small jig with a wiggly plastic tail for my Jitterbug, which was about the tenth lure I had caught bass on that morning. I cast the jig several times and hooked the first Roanoke bass I had ever caught. (The Roanoke bass is native to only a small area.)

Using the same jig, I also caught such fish as bluegill bream, robin redbreast, and some of the biggest crappie I had ever seen. And, of course, I caught several largemouth bass on the jig. Woody outfished me, as he usually does, but I caught my share. We released all of our bass, even the largest ones. I kept a few crappie to bring home for Doris Dale and me to eat.

I regret only one thing about that trip — that I didn't follow Woody's suggestion and take along my fly rod.

At that time, Lake Jordan was less than two years old. It had been heavily stocked, and most of the bass we caught were small. Still, we caught several that weighed four or more pounds. We figured those had been in farm ponds that were flooded when the lake was dammed up. Or that they had been in the Haw River or the New Hope River, which form Lake Jordan.

Lake Jordan was following the pattern of many artificial lakes. The typical new impoundment offers sensational fishing when it is a year or two old. Then the fishing gradually declines until it reaches a normal level of productivity.

Anglers fishing nearby Falls of the Neuse Lake a couple of years later experienced the same kind of fishing. For awhile, both lakes were considered among the country's best for bass fishing. National outdoor magazines publicized the lakes, and it was not unusual to see anglers from as far away as Pennsylvania and New Jersey. But in fishing, as in everything else in life, all good things must come to an end. Fishing declined on both lakes as they began to mature.

Then, after another year or two, both Jordan and Falls of the Neuse lakes entered a second phase of maturity that most other lakes go through. Fishing picked up again. Anglers didn't catch as many bass as they did when the lakes were new, but they did catch more big bass.

True, the December that Woody and I fished Lake Jordan had been abnormally warm, and that may have accounted for the unusual topwater action. But when John Ellison and I went back about a week later, just a few days before Christmas, the weather had turned cool. There was frost on the ground the first few hours we fished, and our breaths formed little clouds of moisture in the chilly air. We still caught a lot of fish, though not as many as Woody and I had caught. And we didn't catch any on topwater lures. But we did catch some on shallow-running lures.

After Lake Jordan's fourth birthday, my partners and I some-times fished the lake without catching a single bass. But I can recall only a few of those trips. Usually we caught something.

I know one thing: While fishing Lake Jordan I lost one of the biggest bass I have ever hung. That happened after the fishing began to decline, about two years after Woody and I had our sensational day. I wouldn't even mention this incident if I hadn't seen the bass and if I didn't have a witness: Bob Suggs, another fishing buddy. Bob and I went to the lake on a steamy-hot June day. Bob, like Woody, is a Greensboro lawyer. I had once hung another big bass while fishing with him on a private lake. When I hooked the fish that time, I was using a fly rod. I apparently had not tied on my bug right, and the bass, after about six jumps, pulled the knot loose. Bob and I both saw the bass. We agreed it weighed about ten pounds.

That was approximately the size of the one I hooked on Lake Jordan that hot June day while again fishing with Bob. Except I hooked the Lake Jordan bass on an artificial worm.

We had been fishing for about two hours without a bump when I pulled the boat into an open spot between some flooded trees and a steep bank. As we drifted down the bank with occasional help from the electric motor, I spotted a log that extended from the bank into the water.

"There's a bass right there," I jokingly said to Bob as I flipped my artificial worm to the end of the log.

I reeled in the slack and felt resistance. I thought I was hung on the log.

"Darn!" I said, or something near to that. "Hung again."

But then the "log" started moving.

First it moved across the bow of the boat. I tried slowing it down. I couldn't. It pulled line out against the drag of my spinning reel.

After the bass — by this time I realized it was not a log — crossed in front of the boat to the other side, I tried fingering the spool of the spinning reel to put a little more pressure on the drag. I didn't want the bass to get to the trees.

My quarry shot out of the water. It seemed to hang there, its side glistening silver in the bright sunlight, for a long time before crashing heavily back into the lake. The bass was within 25 feet of the boat. Bob and I both got a good look at it. It was without a doubt one of the two largest bass I have ever hooked. The bass made several other beautiful leaps, its gills flaring an angry red.

The big fish was so close that we could see the worm hanging in the side of its mouth. Then it began moving toward the trees again. I increased the pressure. The fish jumped again, this time shaking its head with particular violence. The hook shot from its mouth, and I reeled in a line that had only a hook and a sinker on it. The worm was gone.

"I think you're a jinx," I told Bob, one of my best friends, in a shaky voice. "This is the second time this has happened to me while I was fishing with you."

I reached in my shirtpocket for a cigarette. I couldn't find one. For a moment I had completely forgotten that I had quit smoking more than ten years before.

Hanging that big bass was exciting, but not as exciting as something that happened on another trip to Lake Jordan. This time my neighbor Bill Jerome was with me. As we fished the flooded trees near where I had lost that big bass, we saw a large bird swoop down out of a dead pine tree on shore, snare a fish from the water, and glide back to the pine. The bird was too far away to identify.

We fished on. When we were within about 100 feet of the bird, it swooped down to the water again. I saw its brown body and white head and tail. Could it be a rare bald eagle? I borrowed Bill's binoculars and saw that it was, indeed, an eagle. Later, I read that a colony of bald eagles had taken up residence on Lake Jordan.

Seeing that eagle was worth the whole trip. I had fished many days in remote areas of North Carolina without ever seeing an eagle, and here was one of the rarest kinds only a few miles from the bustling state capital of Raleigh.

After I had stopped fishing Lake Jordan regularly, I called Jim Ellis to ask him for advice before making more trips to Jordan. Jim, the manager of a Greensboro fishing tackle store, kept up with the fishing on Lake Jordan. The advice he gave me also applies to the Falls of the Neuse. Here was what Jim suggested:

In the winter, fish a jig with a pork-rind frog or other trailer. When the water warms up to around 50 degrees, switch to spinner baits. As the water gets even warmer, try shallow-running diving lures. Later, use deeper-running lures and artificial worms. In the fall, return to shallow-running lures.

I use topwater lures more than Jim, but I catch fewer fish than he does. It's just that I enjoy topwater fishing as much as a wino loves a free pint of Boone's Farm. Both Jordan and Falls of the Neuse are ideal lakes for topwater fishing when conditions are right. Both lakes are good for fly rods. They have lots of shallow water with flooded bushes, willows, and trees.

Shearon Harris Lake is nearby and is a similar lake that should be fished about like Jordan and Falls of the Neuse.

Lake Jordan covers 13,900 acres and has a 150-mile shoreline. It is on the New Hope and Haw rivers near Pittsboro in Chatham County, and is about 30 miles west of Raleigh and 15 miles south of Durham. Falls of the Neuse Lake covers 12,490 acres and has 230 miles of shoreline. It is in Durham and Wake counties, just northeast of Durham and north of Raleigh, on the Neuse River. Like Jordan, it is a U.S. Army Corps of Engineers lake.

Shearon Harris Lake is just south of Lake Jordan. It is a Carolina Power & Light Company lake. It covers only 4,000 acres and has 40 miles of shoreline.

For information about these lakes, write to these addresses:

B. Everette Jordan Lake
Resource Manager
P.O. Box 144
Moncure, N.C. 27559

Falls of the Neuse Lake
P.O. Box 61068
Neuse Branch
Raleigh, N.C. 27661

Shearon Harris Lake
Carolina Power & Light Co.
P.O. Box 137
New Hill, N.C. 27562

Dale Reed Flickinger with a 9-pound 15-ounce bass caught in the Trent River.

Johnny Horne/Fayetteville Observer

Don Shealy of Fayetteville with a string of Black River bass.

Regis Dandar and the big bass that made him a Tar Heel.

Jim Stratford

Claibourne Darden with one of the largest bass ever caught on a fly rod in Currituck Sound.

Carol Martin

Fishing for bass in the brackish coastland waters of Currituck Sound.

Carol Martin

Stranded in a thick Currituck Sound fog, photographer Carol Martin
and his son-in-law, Larry Moser, were forced to spend the night in a
marsh. Martin used the last shot in his camera to take this photo. During
the night, the wind grew stronger, swamping their boat.

Carol Martin

Dick Doutt (left) and Dave Goforth with two larger-than-average bass from Currituck Sound.

Jim Dean, a widely known outdoors writer, caught these bass—along with a chain pickerel (jack)—in an eastern North Carolina lake. In many North Carolina waters, you never know what you'll catch when you go fishing for bass.

Bob Gooch

Blake Honeycutt prepares to release a bass caught on a North Carolina lake.

Jimmy Harrell displays a pair of sizable largemouth bass.

North Carolina Travel Development Section

Paul Chamblee hauls in a largemouth from Lake Gaston.

Fontana News Bureau

Marshall Wright of Knoxville, Tennessee, with a 10-pound 8-ounce largemouth caught in Fontana Lake in mid-winter.

Fontana News Bureau

Luthur Turpin and a mixed string of largemouth and smallmouth bass and trout caught in Fontana Lake.

Robert W. Watkins

Hubert Greene shows off a 14-pound largemouth and a 7-pound smallmouth caught in Lake Lure.

Buck Paysour

Roger Soles with his limit of Currituck Sound bass caught on a fly rod.
The fly rod is the most effective and most sporting way of catching bass
in the shallow coastal-area waters.

Bodie McDowell/Greensboro Daily News

Believe it or not, the Reverend Sam Sox caught this lunker in a farm pond on a Mepps spinner.

Buck Paysour

Currituck Sound will never be quite the same without the late Wallace O'Neal, for decades an expert guide and fisherman. This photo was taken by the author after a sensational day of fishing with Mr. O'Neal.

Bill Black shows the kind of bass you can catch with an artificial worm if you know how.

Part 3:

Mountain Fishing

High Mountains And Big Bass

Land Of The State Records

Fishing a deep lake surrounded by towering mountains is an awe-inspiring experience. Some of the fish that come from the mountain lakes of North Carolina are also awe-inspiring.

The state-record largemouth and smallmouth bass, along with several other record fish, came from mountain lakes. The record largemouth came out of Santeetlah Reservoir and, according to the N.C. Wildlife Resources Commission, was caught on an L&S Bassmaster lure. The bass weighed 14 pounds 15 ounces. The record smallmouth was caught in Hiwassee Reservoir, not far from where the record largemouth was caught. It weighed 10 pounds 2 ounces.

It is not surprising that the record smallmouth was caught on mountain waters. Just about any angler knows that smallmouth bass prefer cooler waters than their big cousins, the largemouth bass. But the largemouth bass is supposed to thrive better and grow bigger in warm water. Otherwise, why do Florida and California bass get to be such giants?

"Big Leonard" Williams, a genial mountain man, told me he knew better — that largemouth bass grow big in lakes in the mountains of North Carolina. The reason he knew was that he caught that record-shattering largemouth bass. On the same day he caught that fish, he caught two other giants. One of the others weighed 14 pounds 6 ounces. Still another weighed 13 pounds.

Did Big Leonard think his record will ever be broken, and if so, by whom?

"I'll break it," he declared. "I've had a'hold of him. I've had a'hold of two of 'em — one in Fontana and one in Santeetlah."

That didn't sound like bragging to anybody who knew about Big Leonard's other records. At the time he made that comment, he also held the official North Carolina record for walleyed pike and white bass. He caught his record walleye in Santeetlah, too. It weighed 13 pounds 4 ounces. His white bass weighed 4 pounds 15 ounces, and it came from Fontana Reservoir.

Although his walleye and white bass records were later broken, Big Leonard may have been the last person who would ever hold three state freshwater records at one time.

Big Leonard fished all of the Tennessee Valley Authority lakes, but had fished Santeetlah the longest. It backs up to within three-quarters of a mile from where he had lived most of his life. "I've been fishing it ever since the lake was built," he said. "And I fished the river before that."

Big Leonard is typical of mountain people. Like the people of eastern North Carolina, the people of western North Carolina are generally friendly and helpful.

I remember when Hubert Breeze and I pulled my boat to Fontana Lake on a Toyota I then owned. Before leaving Greens-boro, I had the car tuned at one of those bargain places. They didn't tune it right, and the car started overheating on the steep grades west of Asheville. We had to drive a few miles, stop, let the car cool, and then drive a few more miles — all the way to Fontana. When we finally got to Fontana Lake, the little car wouldn't pull my boat out of the water and up the steep ramp to the highway.

Luther Turpin, the Fontana village dock manager, came to our rescue. He sent for his four-wheel drive truck and pulled the boat up the hill for us.

Hubert and I didn't suspect the car's problem was a poor tune-up. Thinking it was something really serious, we took it to a garage at Fontana. The garage owner spent about a half-hour looking at the car, then said all it needed was to be tuned right. He said we should just take it easy going home and then make the people who tuned it the first time do it over again. The garage owner would not charge us.

I told him that if a mechanic in one of the big cities had made that diagnosis, it would have cost me a good part of a day's pay.

"We believe in being neighborly," he replied.

He was right about the tune-up, too. I drove the car several more years after that, and then one of my sons drove it several years. I wish now I had asked the owner of the garage his name.

Another neighborly western North Carolinian, Hubert Greene, shared something in common with Big Leonard Williams. Hubert, too, knew that mountain lakes grow big fish. He had also caught some big bass, both largemouth and smallmouth, when I met him. Although he was one of the great deep-water anglers of our times, Hubert didn't hold any records. But not many people had caught as many big bass as he had caught.

Big Leonard became a guide who was much in demand after word spread of his big fish. Hubert stuck with his boat and motor business.

So if you want to catch a bigger largemouth than Big Leonard's biggest bass — and who doesn't? — you should consider heading for one of the good mountain lakes. You might stand at least a chance of beating the smallmouth record.

Southwestern North Carolina

Chapter 16

Bonefishing For Bass

"If you ever catch a bonefish, you'll forget all about largemouth bass."

Harry Snow Sr. made that prediction just before he started the motor on his skiff to carry Doris Dale and I out to the bonefish flats near Duck Key, Florida. Mr. Snow was described as "one of the world's greatest bonefishing guides" by the late Joe Brooks, a well-known outdoors writer and one of the world's best fly-rod anglers. This was the second time Doris Dale and I had fished with Mr. Snow. The previous trip had been a failure, when measured by the fish we landed. We didn't get a strike. But on this trip, I would finally land my first bonefish.

Notice I said *land*, not *caught*. Doris Dale was the one who actually hooked the bonefish. She was using shrimp for bait, while I was using an artificial fly. After hooking the fish, she thrust her spinning rod at me. I didn't have any choice but to take it. The fish might have gotten away while we argued about who should land it.

There's no doubt about it — the bonefish deserves its reputation as a hard-fighting fish that makes long and fast dashes. The one Doris Dale hooked weighed only about six pounds, but it made at least three sizzling runs of 100 yards or longer. The drag on the spinning reel shrieked. Then the fish began circling the boat so fast I had difficulty keeping a tight line.

The bonefish proved itself a glamorous fish, all right. But not glamorous enough to make me give up my life-long love affair with the freshwater black bass — despite Harry Snow's prediction.

One thing that makes bonefishing intriguing is that it's a combination of stalking, hunting, and fishing. You don't even make a cast until you see a fish, or at least evidence of one. You stand in the boat with the bail of your spinning reel open, or the line of your fly rod stripped, so you can cast immediately when you spot a fish, or a sign of a fish. You wear Polaroid sunglasses and peer through the crystal-clear water looking for a little puff of mud, a fish gliding along, or something else to indicate a fish is there.

Then you cast. Not before.

So what does this have to do with bass fishing in North Carolina?

Believe it or not, there is a section of North Carolina where you sometimes employ similar techniques to catch bass, both largemouth and smallmouth. Except it isn't in shallow water, which is the only place you fish for bonefish in Florida and the Caribbean. Instead, it is in the deep Tennessee Valley Authority (TVA) lakes nestled in the mountains of southwestern North Carolina. I call it "bonefishing for bass."

This method of bass fishing that is similar to bonefishing is used primarily during the summer, when the surface of the water begins to warm. That usually happens around the Fourth of July. It starts at approximately the same time schools of shad begin surfacing in the mountain lakes.

"We change over to Tiny Torpedoes and Skip Jacks and things like that early in the morning for about two hours, and for about two hours in the evening," Luther Turpin told me. "You've got to have your bail — we fish with open-face reels — untripped, and as soon as you see a bass splash out there, you've got to throw out there in just a split second."

You have to cast in a split second because the bass will dive immediately back into the cooler water. They don't like to stay near the top of the water very long.

"But if you're ready to throw right when he jumps and you're within striking distance of him, you'll pretty well get a strike every time," Luther declared.

This unorthodox method is equally effective for largemouth and smallmouth fishing.

"You'll get some big largemouth that way," Luther noted.

When I first met Luther, who is a native of the mountains and an expert angler, he had already fished the TVA lakes for more than 35 years.

"When I first got married, I went to Ohio and worked four years," he recalled. "But I spent more money than I made coming back every weekend to fish. So I decided to just move back."

After returning home, Luther took a job as dock manager at Fontana Village Resort. Over the years, Luther became an authority on fishing, not only at Fontana but also at all the other lakes of southwestern North Carolina: Fontana, Santeetlah, Nantahala, Hiwassee, and Cheoah, and also Chatuge on the North Carolina-Georgia border.

You wouldn't think largemouth bass would grow very large in the cool, deep mountain lakes. Nor would you think topwater fishing would be very good on lakes that deep. But both assumptions would be wrong. Big Leonard Williams's record bass, which weighed 14 pounds 15 ounces, was the largest bass ever caught anywhere in North Carolina — but it wasn't the *only* big bass to come out of the mountain lakes. Some of the largest bass caught in North Carolina each year come from these lakes.

And topwater fishing can be good at the right times of the year. Luther Turpin said he used topwater frequently in the spring. During that season, Rebels, Rapalas, and similar lures often catch fish when used as anglers in the shallow waters of eastern North Carolina use them: popping and twitching across the surface of the water. A fly rod and popping bug is also productive at that time of year.

"You go around and find the pockets with driftwood in them," Luther said. "If you can throw that lure or popping bug two or three inches from the driftwood without getting into it, you're almost sure to get a strike."

The first time I fished Fontana was in mid-June. Most people I talked with said the best things to use were deep-running lures. That's what my younger son, Conrad, and I did for about half a day. We didn't catch anything.

Then I remembered what J.A. King Sr., an avid fly-rod bass fisherman, once told me: "If I'm going to pay the price of admission," he said, "I want to see the picture show."

I picked up my fly rod and tied a deer hair bug on the end of the leader. On about the second cast, I caught a nice smallmouth bass that put on a show worth the price of admission. I caught several other smallmouth that also fought beautifully. Conrad also caught several smallmouth on his spincasting reel and a Tiny Torpedo.

Luther Turpin said he continued to cast topwater lures into July, but used them primarily early in the morning and late in the afternoon. That's when Luther switched from Rebels and Rapalas to Tiny Torpedoes and similar lures, then cast to those swirling bass.

What about the middle of the day in the middle of the summer?

"You get 'em by trolling with just about any kind of deep-running plugs," Luther replied.

Luther said 12-pound test is the smallest size line that's practical for trolling, and that heavier line is even better. You should bump the lure along the bottom, even at the risk of getting hung up in the stumps and tree tops that cover much of the bottoms of the TVA lakes.

Night fishing, especially with a Jitterbug thrown close to the bank, can be very good in mid-summer. "They get a lot of big fish that way," Luther said.

Even in late spring and early summer, night fishing can be good on the TVA lakes. However, most anglers use big hump-backed Rebels and similar lures in the mouths of creeks, where the water is clear and only about six to eight feet deep.

In the early fall, after the water begins to cool, topwater lures are once again good for daytime topwater fishing. "You can do pretty good on topwater then by just throwing it out there and letting it lie a long time, and then giving it a little twitch," Luther said.

Trolling becomes effective once again in October. Luther said he liked to use homemade jigs in the late fall and through the winter. "If I had to fish with one thing the year around, I'd fish a Doll fly made out of bucktail," he declared. "I like the eighth-ounce Doll flies and eight-pound test line."

Luther said he fished right through the winter, often taking his fishing tackle with him when he goes hunting. "It gets real cold," he admitted. "We have to wear insulated boots."

He told about one particular December fishing trip when he was using his Doll fly. "I...caught my limit of smallmouth bass off one point. I mean, it was just one after the other."

Natural bait is also good in the winter, as well as in the dog days of summer, especially for inexperienced anglers, Luther said. "In the hot summer, in the middle of the day, you park your boat on one of the points and use a night crawler or a minnow with a BB shot, and just throw it out there and let it sink down, and leave it three or four minutes," he said. "If you don't get a strike, you just wind it in and throw it out again."

He added, however, that an experienced angler can usually catch more fish on artificial lures than on natural bait.

You can catch both largemouth and smallmouth bass on the TVA lakes using any of Luther's methods. But if you're fishing for smallmouth bass exclusively, you should use smaller lures and smaller line than you'd normally use for largemouth. The smallmouth is known for its energetic leaps.

"The first thing a smallmouth does when he is hooked is to come out of the water at least one time," Luther observed. "The larger ones will come up three or four times."

He said a smallmouth will make itself known immediately when it's hooked on natural bait. "As soon as you set the hook, you'll see the line start coming up. I generally tell the fisherman to watch out, that the fish is about to come out of the water. Then he comes out."

What about artificial worms on the TVA lakes?

"Artificial worms don't do too good in these lakes," Luther said. "I've guided a lot of people who really believe in them. But they just don't work up here. I've had people who used them, and I've used my stuff, and I've caught fish, and they haven't."

Luther said he didn't know why the bass grow so big in the mountain lakes, but he suspected it was because there is such a plentiful supply of shad and other food all year.

Good anglers, including Luther, vary the color of lures they use on the mountain lakes, just as they do on other waters. Luther said he preferred yellow or brown lures in dingy water, and brown Doll flies in dark water. "When the water is clear, I like white, especially in the late afternoon."

On clear days, light-colored lures are usually the best.

"On a day like today, I like black or purple, or black with some white in it," he said. That day was dark, rain was falling, and clouds obscured the mountain tops.

The consensus among fly-rod anglers who often fish the TVA lakes is that black, or black with some yellow, are the best colors to use.

Luther said he rarely used a depth finder or a temperature gauge. "The TVA keeps up with the water temperature, so we pretty well know what it is all the time," he explained. "And we boys who fish these lakes all the time know what the depth is at different places." But he added that a depth finder would help a person who is not familiar with the lakes.

As you might expect, Luther ranked Fontana as the best of the TVA lakes for bass fishing. But he conceded that all of the TVA lakes are excellent. Fontana often shows up in fishing magazine surveys as one of the nation's best fishing lakes. At least one of the neighboring lakes is usually mentioned, too.

The accommodations at Fontana Lake are excellent and reasonably priced. For information, write:

Fontana Village Resort
Fontana Dam, N.C. 28733

There are many fine restaurants and lodgings in towns within driving distance of the other TVA lakes. All you need is a road map to find a town close to the lake you plan to fish. Or you can stay at Fontana Village and still be relatively close to all of the lakes. Boats are available to rent at most places. You may also want to hire a guide, especially for your first trip.

"A good fisherman can fish these lakes on his own and catch fish," Luther Turpin said. "But a guide knows where the hot spots are."

Rates for guides are reasonable when compared to many other parts of the country. "The guides fish, too," Luther said. "If they didn't, they'd probably charge a lot more."

If you fish on your own, you can obtain a map at the boat dock at Fontana or from other sources. Mountain people help make mountain fishing pleasurable. Most, like Luther Turpin, are friendly, so don't hesitate to ask for advice and help.

After I landed that Florida bonefish, I asked Doris Dale why she insisted on passing her rod to me after hooking the fish.

"I knew that catching one made a difference to you," she said. "It didn't to me."

You see now why our marriage has lasted so long.

Wonder what would happen if she ever snagged a bass large enough to shatter Big Leonard Williams's record....

Lake Lure, Lake Thorpe, And Others

Chapter 17

Pretty Lakes And Good Fishing

It was a crisp fall day when Hubert Greene and his wife, Rose, set out to fish Lake Lure in an old johnboat. Hubert, one of the country's best deep-water anglers, was using a spinner bait. They had been out a couple of hours when they saw Jake Wilson and Bill McClain, who were also fishing from a boat.

"Hey, Hubert!" Jake yelled, "How about showing us how you use that spinner bait."

Hubert flipped the spinner bait over toward Jake and Bill's boat. "I was casting it out and letting it sink to the bottom," Hubert later recalled. "It had already hit the bottom."

Just as Hubert began his retrieve, something walloped the spinner bait. Soon, Hubert realized he was tied into a bigger than average bass. And he didn't even have a landing net. Hubert and Rose were residents of Lake Lure, and they didn't bother to bring a net because they were just out for a few hours of fun.

As Hubert and the bass battled, Bill and Jake drew their boat closer to Hubert's boat and passed over a net. Soon afterward, Hubert finally led the bass — a largemouth — to the net and landed it.

Later that day, Hubert weighed the bass on a set of certified scales. The scales registered exactly 14 pounds.

"We weighed it every way we could," Hubert said later as a smile spread across his sun-bronzed face. "But we just couldn't get it to go more than that."

Although the bass wasn't a state record, it was one of the largest ever caught in North Carolina. On the same outing, Hubert caught a seven-pound smallmouth. That's a mighty big smallmouth, too.

Although the 14-pound largemouth was the largest bass Hubert ever caught, it wasn't a fluke. Catching big bass is a habit with Hubert. He was once the subject of a magazine article after catching 27 bass in one year that weighed more than eight pounds each.

Hubert built a reputation over the years as a good all-around angler, but the thing he is best known for is deep-water fishing for both largemouth and smallmouth bass. In other words, the kind of fishing you find around Lake Lure. Even before he caught that 14-pounder, he contended that Lake Lure offered some of the best bass fishing in the North Carolina mountains. But he admitted it wasn't always so good.

"Lake Lure was one of the top lakes in the state a long time ago," he said. "After that, it fell off some. But I think it is coming back."

Hubert's fishing success backed up that comment. Just a few weeks before he caught the 14-pound largemouth and the 7-pound smallmouth, he landed another smallmouth that weighed more than 7 pounds. "I got home about 30 minutes before dark," he recalled. "As I usually do, I went out and chucked a few before dark. On that, day, right off, *Bam!*"

That smallmouth was no fluke, either. Jim Ledbetter of Hickory, one of Hubert's friends, once came to Lake Lure to visit Hubert. Jim, also a good angler, was the host of an outdoors program on a local TV station.

"We went out and fished awhile," Hubert recalled. "Then we came back in and had a warm lunch and watched a football game a little. [Hubert used to play football at Clemson University and even had some professional prospects when an unfortunate injury cut short his career.] Then we went back down to the dock and threw off the dock, and *Wham!* I caught an eight-pound smallmouth."

So you can see why Hubert argued that Lake Lure was making a comeback. A deep lake, Lure is usually clear. But the water can vary from green to indigo blue, depending on such things as the weather and how many boats are stirring up the water.

Many people think Lake Lure is the prettiest lake in North

Carolina. It is at the feet of several mountains, including spectacular Rumbling Bald with its sheer granite face.

As you might expect, a resort-area lake as beautiful as Lake Lure is sometimes crowded. The lake has many homes and cottages on its shores and is frequented by tourists. Happily, however, the best fishing seasons are during months when the tourists and water skiers have all but deserted the lake.

"During June, July, and August, we have a lot of tourists," Hubert said. "Our best fishing is usually February until April or May, and sometimes into June. And September, October, and November are real good. August is good, too, but there are a lot of tourists here then."

What advice could he offer about how to fish Lake Lure?

"Right now, in the fall, when the temperature begins to drop, the fish start to move on the banks," Hubert said. "In the morning, the banks will be cool. But in the afternoon, they'll be just as warm as they were before. So when they cool off in the morning, I'll go to the banks with a topwater or a spinner bait. Then during the day, about noon or so, it seems like they disappear. So you've got to go back to the structure with worms.

"This will hold true until the water cools off, and then after it cools off, to say about 60 degrees, many of the fish will come back into the shallow water and stay somewhere around the 10- to 15-foot range. Also, when the water is cool on the banks, swimming lures are good, as are crankbaits."

When Hubert used a topwater bait, whether in the fall or the spring, he usually chose the Crazy Shad. That lure has propellers on the front and back. The Devils Horse and similar lures can also be good, but Hubert said he just liked the way the Crazy Shad cast.

He agreed, though, that topwater fishing was not as good as in years past. "I think it's because there is more traffic now, and the fish stay a little deeper."

How about later in the year, say in winter? What lures did he suggest then?

"We use spinner baits all winter," he answered. "We'll go to spoons sometimes, too."

The spoons he suggested included the Hopkins or Salty Dogs.

He said he usually jigged them at a depth of up to 20 to 25 feet, deeper than he fished under most other circumstances. "I fish most of the time at from 5 to 15 feet." The only exceptions were those times when he used spoons and topwater baits.

Hubert liked to use crankbaits sometimes in the winter, fishing them primarily in submerged tree tops, which are also among his favorite places to fish spinner baits. He continued using spinner baits when the water warmed a little, usually in March.

"We also use crankbaits a lot then, especially the Hellbenders and Water Dogs and such things as Bagley's Balsa B's," he said.

The spinner bait is good all year, except during the hot summer on Lake Lure and nearby lakes, Hubert said. "I usually fish the spinner bait slow. I've caught more fish using it that way. I like to fish it in the tree tops. You let it come over the limbs, and after it comes over a limb, you let it fall a little ways. A lot of times, the bass will hit it right then."

He said he used a chartreuse-colored spinner bait most of the time, even when fishing in crystal-clear water.

"I fish Nantahala a lot, and you can see a spinner bait 20 to 25 feet deep, and you'll be looking at it, and all of a sudden you'll see it disappear. You won't see the fish, just your spinner bait disappearing."

Later in the spring, when the water approached 65 degrees Fahrenheit, Hubert sometimes switched to topwater lures and to the artificial worm again. His favorite colors in worms? Blue, when the water is stained or dingy.

"Black and red are hard to beat under almost any conditions," he said. "But in crystal-clear water, I use red. Sometimes when the water gets real green-looking, I catch a lot on the black grape worm."

Many anglers think large-size lines frighten bass. Hubert had a different theory. He concluded that larger-diameter lines cut down on the number of strikes only because they act as a drag on a lure, making it act and look unnatural. So an angler has to do something to compensate.

In Hubert's judgment, the best way to counteract the drag is to use a reel with a spool that runs smoothly. He said he almost always used free-spool baitcasting reels with 20-pound test line when possible. When he was forced to use light lines, he switched to an ultralight spincasting reel. The reason he loaded his reels with 20-pound line whenever possible was that lighter line wears out quickly.

"I've always got my eyes on the line," he said of worm fishing. "I watch it right where it goes into the water. Sometimes, when you get a hit, you will see the line moving. Sometimes it will start moving and then stop. I set the hook pretty hard. I set it more or less like a shock treatment."

A fluorescent line is more visible for this type of fishing.

Hubert and his fishing buddies decided long ago not to even take the time to reel in the slack before setting the hook. "We just jerk," Hubert explained. "It's like cracking a whip. A quick snap is better than a pull."

Hubert caught his second-biggest largemouth bass, which weighed 11 pounds 7 ounces, on an artificial worm in Lake James. In fact, he said, he has caught more fish on artificial worms over the years than on any other type of lure.

The year he gained national attention by boating the 27 bass that weighed over eight pounds each, he caught about half of them on artificial worms. About 35 percent were caught on spinner baits. A few struck topwater lures. The others succumbed to crankbaits or swimming lures.

When I first met Hubert, he had caught a number of bass that weighed nine pounds or more. One ten-pound largemouth had eaten a squirrel before it hit his lure.

When bass are hitting surface lures on Lake Lure, some people use fly rods and popping bugs. "Most of them use the Peck's Poppers," Hubert said.

Some fly rodders use underwater streamers when fish want subsurface lures. The streamers are sometimes deadly, especially on smallmouth bass.

Most of the time, you can catch smallmouth bass using the same strategy you use for largemouth on Lake Lure. In fact, you often catch both smallmouth and largemouth on the same lures. However, Hubert said he tended to use smaller lures for smallmouth than for largemouth. He still caught some largemouth on the smaller lures, but not as many.

The smallmouth is a sensational fighter. During a fight, it always comes to the top and cavorts and showers spray all over the place — no matter how far down in the water it was when it was hooked.

"December is one of the better months for smallmouth," Hubert said. "The Little George is good. You go the tree tops. We also use bucktails or crappie jigs for them."

The bucktails and crappie jigs are similar to the lures Luther Turpin makes for use on Fontana Lake. Hubert, however, said he avoided using crappie jigs when possible. "I like a jig big enough so that when I pull it, I can feel it," he explained. "Sometimes when a bass hits a real little jig, you won't hang him, because you will hardly know when he hits. The jigs that are a little heavier will keep your line a little tighter."

Hubert described a method of fishing for swirling largemouth and smallmouth that was similar to "bonefishing for bass" on Fontana Lake (See Chapter 16). But instead of using topwater lures as Luther Turpin used for swirling bass, Hubert used Hopkins spoons. "We throw it out and let it fall under them," Hubert said. "I flip the spoon there, and just as soon as it hits the water, I get ready."

He agreed with Luther that the bass won't stay on the surface of the water very long, but will immediately dive back to the more comfortable cool water near the bottom. "Most of the time, they will go to the bottom and swim in figure eights until they come back up again."

When bass swirl on top, Hubert said he liked to work the Hopkins spoon just under the surface most of the time. But if the fish refused to hit the spoon, he let the spoon fall all the way to the bottom. That way, the bass would see it even when they returned to deep water after their brief expeditions to the surface.

When I first met him, Hubert had placed in the top ten in a number of tournaments, although his thriving boat and motor business kept him from fishing as much as many other tournament anglers. Nevertheless, he had won so many local tournaments he had lost count.

If you'd like to try to duplicate Hubert's success on Lake Lure, you can launch at one of the excellent public boat ramps on the lake or at a marina owned by Hubert's company. You need a special fishing permit and a special boat permit to fish Lake Lure; you get these from the town clerk.

Hubert's tactics will catch fish on all of the North Carolina mountain lakes, but Hubert said he especially enjoyed fishing Lake Thorpe, near Cashiers. "It's a small lake," he said, "but it's a real good lake. It's got a lot of fingers and a few cottages on it. It's also got a lot of largemouth and smallmouth bass."

The riprap is a good place to fish on Lake Thorpe. (Riprap is created by dumping rocks around the shoreline to keep it from eroding. Sometimes, rocks settle naturally around the edge of the water.)

"The fish, especially smallmouth bass, come up to the riprap to feed on crawfish," Hubert explained.

Hubert said that a good bait for that type of fishing is the spinner bait, or a diving bait similar to the Balsa B. It should be brown or another color similar to that of a crawfish. He said he liked the balsa baits because the splat they make when they hit the water is more natural than the noise created by lures made of most other materials.

According to Hubert, the best way to fish the riprap is to cast straight to it from the boat, rather than ahead of the boat. "A lot of times, you have a partner in the boat who wants to sail his lure ahead of you," Hubert said. "He's just cutting himself off. If he throws directly to the bank and lets it fall down the riprap, he is fishing from zero to say ten feet. That fish can be anywhere in that range." Hubert made an imaginary cast in front of an imaginary boat and continued. "But if he throws over there, by the time he comes away from it, he's lost the chance to fish all depths."

Except for these special techniques, Hubert said Lake Thorpe should be fished about like you would fish any other mountain lake.

Hubert said he liked to fish South Carolina lakes, too, especially those in the mountains. He said one good lake of that type is

Lake Jocassee. Several arms of Jocassee extend into North Carolina. Since South Carolina and North Carolina do not have reciprocal fishing license agreements, North Carolinians must buy nonresident licenses to fish the South Carolina portion of the lake.

"It's a mountain lake and is crystal clear," Hubert said. "You've got to fish it pretty deep, 25 or 30 feet about 90 percent of the time."

Hubert described a special technique he used for fishing a spinner bait on Jocassee, a technique that can be used successfully on just about any deep lake. You cast your spinner bait (or any other sinking lure you may be using) and let it fall. Many times, a bass will hit the lure while it's falling. "If he hits it at a certain depth on the way down, after that I start retrieving when the spinner bait hits that depth."

You can, of course, count to yourself to determine how deep your spinner bait is when the bass hits it. After that, you begin retrieving on that count on every cast you make. Hubert said you might even want to switch to a lure that runs at the depth at which the bass first hit your sinking bait.

Most of the time, he said, all bass will hit at the same depth. That's one reason why many successful anglers use a depth finder on mountain lakes.

"A lot of days," Hubert said, "we'll go to the banks and start working out. When we find the fish, we'll find our depths. Say today, we find the fish at 25 feet on a point or underwater island or other structure that's 25 feet deep...When you establish that — it will take you a little time to establish it — it will usually hold true for all day."

But Hubert added a word of caution: "Now tomorrow, when you come back, it may be different."

So you just have to repeat the process the next time you go fishing.

Hubert said that a person could fish the mountain lakes in just about any stable boat they have available. "A bass boat just makes fishing more comfortable," he said. "At Lake Lure lately, I've been using an aluminum johnboat and a ten-horsepower motor, and we're catching just as many fish."

But he repeated his advice about the necessity of using a depth finder. "A depth finder is particularly important in finding the points. When you see a point that seems to come straight out, it may turn. So I try to find the end of it and sometimes drop a marker. Then I'll go over to the side, and I'll cast on top of the point. I'll cast shallow. I'll cast deep. I'll cast across it. It takes a little time to go through this, but if you'll do it, you'll catch a lot more fish."

One other lake on which Hubert Greene's tactics can be deadly is the Kerr Scott Reservoir near North Wilkesboro.

Hubert confessed that he didn't know why the bass grow so big in the mountains. "You know," he said, "that about all of the state's freshwater records are held in western North Carolina."

One of his theories was that the water is purer and less polluted, and there is less fishing in the mountains than in some other parts of the state.

If you decide to fish Lake Thorpe, there are at least two convenient ramps. Both are on the road that runs from Cashiers to the lake. One ramp is behind a service station, and the other is near a church.

There are plenty of motels and good restaurants near all the mountain lakes. You can just look at a map and decide which town you want to be in or near. Then, for a list of motels and hotels, you can contact a travel agent, the Chamber of Commerce in that town, or the Travel Section of the Department of Natural and Economic Resources in Raleigh. You should make reservations as far in advance as possible, especially during the tourist season.

River Smallmouth

Chapter 18

Are Bass Anglers Getting Soft?

We bass anglers are getting soft. At least most of us. We sit on soft cushions as we flit from place to place in our big bass boats, and we're equipped with electric-powered anchors, electric-start gasoline engines, power motor lifts, drive-on boat trailers, and foot-controlled electric trolling motors — all designed to make it unnecessary for us to use many of our muscles.

We peer at the face of electronic gadgets whose winking lights tell us how deep and how warm or cool the water is. Some bass boats are even equipped with small computers that tell us what color lures to use.

"My husband's boat has so many electrical things on it," one woman said only half-jokingly, "that he is afraid to get it wet."

We tend to shun the cold, shallow, fast-moving mountain streams where smallmouth bass fishing is difficult but often fantastic.

Tommy Osborne, a retired game warden who lived in Watauga County, thought that was a shame.

I met Mr. Osborne through Walter Edmisten, retired District 7 supervisor for the N.C. Wildlife Resources Commission's Protection and Enforcement Division. That district includes 11 western North Carolina counties. Mr. Edmisten was Mr. Osborne's boss. But the two men were life-long friends and remained friends after they retired.

When I visited Mr. Edmisten's home just outside Boone to talk about river smallmouth bass fishing, I thought I was going to talk only to Mr. Edmisten. But he had obligingly asked Mr. Osborne to sit in. "Tommy knows as much about smallmouth fishing as anybody I know," Mr. Edmisten said.

Naturally, my first question was: Where are the best places to

169

fish for bass in rivers in the Boone area?

"For smallmouth," Mr. Edmisten replied, "I'd say it is definitely the South Fork of the New River." He said the North Fork downstream, along with the New River itself, offered good smallmouth bass fishing.

"Is that right, Tommy?" Mr. Edmisten turned to Mr. Osborne.

"That's right," Mr. Osborne agreed.

What is the best way to fish that water?

"You can wade it or float it," Mr. Osborne answered. "You need a rubber raft to fish it after you get down in Ashe County, because it gets to be a pretty good size down there."

Some people use canoes on the river. "But they are not for me," Mr. Osborne declared. He said he didn't like canoes because he thought they were too unstable. Nor did he like the idea of fishing the river in a flat-bottomed boat. "It's too rocky in most places," he said. "You'd bust the bottom out."

Mr. Edmisten continued his list of rivers that are good for smallmouth bass fishing. "Then we have the Watauga River over here flowing west. It goes into Tennessee, and it's also good for smallmouth."

How do you fish that river?

"You wade it mostly," Mr. Osborne responded. "You've got falls that drop down suddenly over steep rock cliffs. I don't think you'd want to go down over those kinds of drops in a rubber raft."

Or a canoe, he could have said.

"The New River is your best bet," he added. "You go down below Jefferson where Highway 16 crosses it, and then from there on down to the Virginia line. You can go down to where 221 crosses it if you want to, and all that section in there is good. That's where you often catch your best bass, where 221 crosses it."

The mountain rivers hold few largemouth bass, but both men agreed that an angler could catch a stray one occasionally.

Mr. Osborne's favorite lure for river smallmouth fishing was the Flatfish in the small sizes. He thought the wood Flatfish had the best action. He also enjoyed success with the Heddon shallow-running River Runt lure, again in the small sizes. Other lures he mentioned were the jointed L&S Mirrolures and spinners like the

Mepps, Rooster Tail, and Panther Martin.

"Topwater can be good, too," he said. "In fact, about any small lure that runs shallow and has good action will catch smallmouth bass. Action is the main thing."

Mr. Edmisten and Mr. Osborne agreed that spring and summer are good times to fish for smallmouth bass. Mr. Osborne said, "I'd rather fish when the water gets warm: June, July, and August. That's because it's more comfortable to wade."

But to catch big fish, he said, you should fish in the fall. "The prettiest string of smallmouth I ever caught was in the fall. The reason I remember it so well was it was on the last day of the last game of the World Series between St. Louis and the Yankees...That's been a long time. I caught seven that day — I never weighed them, but the smallest one was 16 inches long. The fellow with me, Lee Stout, caught two little ones. I rode with him, and he was about not to let me ride back."

Mr. Edmisten and Mr. Osborne said you can use the same methods of fishing for smallmouth in the North Carolina mountain rivers no matter what time of year you fish.

When it comes to lure colors, there is no difference in large-mouth and smallmouth bass fishing: You should use dark lures in dingy water and on dark days, and light lures on light days and in clear water. You won't have the problem of muddy water very often, though; most mountain rivers clear up fast after a rain.

Many anglers think that live bait, especially lizards and minnows, is the best bait for river smallmouth bass. "Really, your best bet for smallmouth would be live minnows," Mr. Edmisten said. "That's their natural food, and if a man just wanted to catch bass, that's what he should use."

Mr. Osborne concurred. "That's right. I remember when I'd take my brother down to the New River in Ashe County. There used to be a little old dam over there. My brother would fish below the dam with worms and an old jerk pole and catch those little horny heads about this big" — Mr. Osborne held up his finger and thumb to indicate the minnows were about an inch long — "and he'd swing them up to me, and I'd put them on a hook and catch bass."

You have to fish live bait differently than artificial bait, however. "Most of the time," Mr. Osborne said, "a river smallmouth will hit an artificial so hard, he'll hang himself. But it's still a good idea to help him a little."

With live bait, on the other hand, you have to exercise some patience and set the hook when the time is right. "When a smallmouth bass first hits a minnow, he will run a little ways and then stop," Mr. Osborne explained. "You wait until he takes off again, then you set the hook, because he has turned that minnow around. They always swallow the minnow first."

That must be a trait shared by many species of fish. Several years after I talked with Mr. Osborne and Mr. Edmisten, I fished Kerr Lake with Bill Black and Taylor Turner, an expert on striped bass fishing. It was the first time I ever used minnows for stripers. When I got my first thump, Taylor cautioned me to wait until the fish hit the minnow again. "In the interval, he's turning the minnow around," Taylor said.

I waited and was rewarded, after a battle, with a gleaming striped bass that weighed 12 pounds. That day, we caught 11 striped bass that weighed an average of almost 10 pounds each.

But don't use a bobber when fishing with minnows for smallmouth bass in mountain rivers. Use a small split shot instead.

"I like to cast out at the head of the pool and let the minnow wash around the pool," Mr. Osborne said. He liked the center of the pool best, whether he was fishing live or artificial bait. He let his minnow drift from the head of the pool to the middle. The center, he said, is where the bass usually hit.

"Your smallmouth is most like any other fish," he said. "He has a hiding place...Smallmouth don't stay up there [at the head of the pool] to catch food as it comes into the hole. I think they figure they can stay...15 to 20 feet into the pool and catch it anyhow."

After a smallmouth bass is hooked it puts on a fine show, whether you catch him on live or artificial bait. "You won't hook one hardly without him breaking the water," Mr. Edmisten noted.

"I've seen them go across the water 30 or 40 feet just tearing the water up," Mr. Osborne added.

Just about any type of tackle can be used for smallmouth, But

Mr. Osborne preferred spincasting gear. He and Don Shealy, the great shallow-water bass specialist from Fayetteville, agreed on that point.

"I have caught 18-pound stripers on my closed-face reel," said Mr. Osborne, an all-around good angler. Using his spincasting tackle, he once caught eight largemouth bass that weighed a total of 44 pounds while sitting in one spot on Lake Norman. He used lizards for bait. "I had a live box in the boat," he recalled. "I'd catch seven bass, and then I'd look at them to see if I had one smaller. If I did, I'd put one from the live box back in the water and replace it with one larger. I quit at four o'clock. My arms were so tired I had to quit."

Mr. Osborne gave up fishing the mountain rivers for largemouth as the years caught up with him. "It's harder to fish a river than it is to fish a lake," he observed. "On a lake, you sit there in comfort in a boat. In the rivers, even if you have a rubber raft, you've got to get out and pull it around certain places. And you've got to paddle it. I've been on the New River in a rubber raft down near the Virginia-North Carolina line in Allegheny County in a big long hole, and me and another guy would be just paddling as hard as we could, and the wind would be blowing us back up."

You can catch smallmouth in the lower reaches of almost all of the North Carolina mountain rivers by using the methods Mr. Osborne and Mr. Edmisten recommended for the New River. However, the upper reaches usually contain few smallmouth. The upper reaches are, for the most part, trout waters.

As an example, Mr. Edmisten cited the South Fork of the New River where it crosses Highway 421 at Boone. "Right there, you might catch lunker trout," he said. "You would catch bass farther east of Boone."

The South Fork and North Fork are both good smallmouth rivers in the lower reaches. They join to form the New River, the river that became a national cause when environmentalists successfully prevented a power company from building a dam on it.

Mr. Edmisten said he had a theory about why bass fishing is not very good in stretches of rivers that contain trout. "Your bass in trout water, what few there are, are all small. Your trout water is too cold for a bass to grow to be any size."

In addition, there's usually an area between the two types of water where neither bass fishing nor trout fishing is very good. "It's almost too warm for trout and not quite warm enough to make a bass grow much," Mr. Edmisten explained. "That's what they call the marginal water."

One pleasant thing about most smallmouth bass rivers: They aren't crowded, especially if you can fish them during a weekday. But they're just about all located close to resort areas. So if you plan to fish them during the tourist season, you should make motel, hotel, or campground reservations before setting out.

A word of warning: Not only are many mountain rivers difficult to fish, but they are also among the most dangerous waters in the state. It doesn't make much difference whether you are floating the rivers or wading them — one wrong move and you could slip beneath the water and bang your head or body against the rocks. Either way, it could be the end of your fishing. So unless you know what you're doing, fish these streams at your own risk.

Part 4:

Special Techniques For Fishing North Carolina

Bugging
The
Bass

Chapter 19

A Hundred Bass A Day?

It wasn't an ideal morning, especially for using a fly rod. The sky was dark and rain was falling. The wind blew so hard it created a chop on Currituck Sound and bent the marsh reeds until their tops almost touched the water. Yet Roger Soles had already caught more than his limit of bass on his fly rod.

Even now, he was bringing in a bass that looked about 15 inches long. Roger unhooked the bass and put it back in the water. Then he turned to me, seated in the back of the boat, and insisted, "Here, you move up here."

We made the switch. But Roger continued to catch about four bass for every one I landed. Roger, as he almost always does when he is fishing for bass, was using his reed-thin fly rod. On this day, I was using a baitcasting outfit. I enjoy using a fly rod, but trying to cast a popping bug into the wind had convinced me to switch.

The kind of skill Roger demonstrated that day was what inspired people who had fished with him to agree that he was the best fly-rod fisherman they had ever seen. Even professional guides said that. The late Grover Cleveland Sawyer, a famous Currituck Sound guide, said he had never fished with a fly-rod fisherman as good as Roger. Mr. Sawyer's son, G.C., also a veteran guide, said much the same thing.

Wallace O'Neal, my friend who guided on Currituck Sound longer then anybody else, fished with Roger one day. "He's the best I've ever seen," proclaimed Mr. O'Neal, who had guided for some nationally known fly-rod anglers.

One morning after Roger and I fished with veteran Currituck

177

guide Bill Smith for the first time, Bill stopped for lunch at one of the few shelters on the east side of the sound, the Piney Island Club dock. Many of the guides gathered there each day at noon to eat lunch and compare notes. On that day, the guides formed a little knot away from the anglers.

"I tell you one thing," I overhead Bill say, "I've got a fly fisherman today I'd put up against anybody I've ever fished with."

Happily, you don't have to be as skilled as Roger Soles to catch bass on a fly rod. On many days, even an average fly rodder can outfish people using other tackle — especially on the shallow eastern North Carolina creeks, rivers, and sounds. Despite the common misconception about the difficulty of learning to use a fly rod, almost anybody with average intelligence and coordination can learn to use one well enough to catch at least some bass.

I'm not in the league with Roger or some of my other friends. But not long after I learned to use a fly rod, a party of eight caught only 50 bass in two days of fishing on Currituck Sound, and I caught 36 of the 50. I was the only one in the group using a fly rod.

You would be safe 90 days out of 100 if you bet on Roger Soles against any other angler using baitcasting or spinning gear on coastal-area fresh and brackish water. The fly rod and a popping bug in the hands of an expert like Roger will also catch bass in other parts of the state during the spring and fall, or early in the morning and late in the afternoon even in the summer.

Over the years, I fished Currituck Sound about 12 times or a total of 24 fishing days with Roger. He caught and released more than his limit of bass on every trip except two — and there was little water in the sound on those trips. On at least eight days, he released more than 60 bass. On several days, I quit counting after he had landed more than 100 bass.

Why are the fly rod and popping bug — the only lure many fly rodders now use for bass — so potent in shallow fresh and brackish water? I once asked Roger that question.

One explanation, he said, is that a bass bug is small and light compared to spinning or baitcasting lures. "A bass bug hits the water more softly. It sounds more life-like."

The heavier baitcasting or spinning lures, Roger noted, often make a bass nervous. A bass will run off about five or six feet after the bait hits the water. Then the bass will turn and watch. If you wait a while before twitching the lure, you often will be rewarded with a strike.

You don't have to go through all this when using a fly rod, Roger noted. The gentle splat a fly-rod bug makes when it hits the water doesn't scare the bass.

"A lot of times, a bass will strike the bug as soon as it hits the water. You've even seen them come out of the water to get a bass bug before the bug even hits the water."

That is true. It's a thrilling sight to see a bass shoot out of the water like a small rocket to wallop a popping bug while the bug is still 12 inches above the water. I've never seen a bass do that to get to a baitcasting or spinning lure.

One of the remarkable things about Roger is that he didn't even take up bass fishing until he was an adult. Even then, he didn't have as much time to fish as do most other good fly rodders. As a young business executive destined to become president and chief executive officer of Jefferson-Pilot Corporation, he had other fish to fry, so to speak. But he approached fishing just as he approached everything else — whether it was golf, raising money for charity, or running a corporation. He did it with a zeal that precluded even a hint of failure.

Roger taught me how to use a fly rod in his backyard while his wife, Majelle, and Doris Dale were socializing. A few days later, *Greensboro News & Record* outdoors writer Bodie McDowell showed me how to do the "double haul" in the newspaper's parking lot. The double haul is a method that helps you quickly shoot out a line. It also adds power to your cast, making it easier to cast into the teeth of a high wind. But it was Roger I sought to pattern my fly rod style after. While fishing with him, I watched what he did and followed his advice as closely as I could.

I noticed that Roger and the other good fly rodders I knew used smaller bugs than suggested by the experts who write for national magazines. The bug Roger showed me the day he taught me to use a fly rod was a Number 6 bug. Later, when I fished with Roger, he caught both bass and bream on the same bug.

Roger always pulled the rubber legs off of the bugs he bought. When he bought bugs at the old Phipps Hardware basement in Greensboro, he jokingly asked manager Ralph Clark for a discount; he said he shouldn't have to pay for the rubber legs he pulled off.

"They just seem to work better for me without the rubber legs," he told me. "I think they pop a little better."

I also noticed that Roger usually fished his bass bugs in spurts. Without the rubber legs, the bugs looked like miniature Devils Horses coming through the water.

Another thing I learned by watching Roger was that it is best to start out the day fishing a bass bug relatively slowly. If that doesn't work, fish more aggressively — especially when there is a ripple on the water.

"I use whatever it takes to interest the fish," Roger told me.

I observed early that Roger had quick reflexes. He set the hook instantly when he got a strike. His line was always tight. He rarely lost a fish he hooked.

Even a small bug is difficult to fish in the wind, because it has much more wind resistance than a small trout fly. Yet on the windy days I fished with Roger, he made it look easy. He continued to use his fly rod when small-craft warning flags had been hoisted along the coast.

He once amazed newspaper publisher Carmage Walls of Houston, Texas, by catching fish on a fly rod while fishing Currituck Sound on a day when a hurricane was roaring just off the nearby Outer Banks.

On one windy day, I asked him what his secret was.

He was surprised I hadn't already noticed. "I fish it side arm," he said. "I try to fish it close to the water where the wind is not so strong. I try to cast under the wind as much as possible."

But sometimes, he bulled a popping bug into the wind by sheer force.

He told me the first cast with a popping bug was the most important and will usually get a bass if there's one around, even if the cast is off the mark by several feet. Yet I had seen him cast five or six times when the wind was blowing hard — the only times he had to make more than one cast to hit a target — to get to a small pocket. About the time I had decided there couldn't possibly be a bass around, Roger would hit the pocket, and often a bass would boil up and engulf the bug.

Didn't that contradict his theory about the first cast being the most important?

"When there is a chop on the water, and the water has already been disturbed, that's different," Roger admitted.

Another fishing friend who is a great fly rodder, Claibourne Darden Sr., showed me a trick he used when the wind is blowing hard: He shortened his leader. That way, the power is transmitted to the bug more quickly, he said. Claibourne agreed with Roger that when the water is already disturbed, there is less danger of the line frightening the fish.

I have seen Claibourne fish with a leader that was no more than two feet long. Those were days when I had long since given up on the fly rod because my arm was sore from trying to punch a bug into the wind.

Claibourne, too, taught me a lot about fly-rod fishing. He agreed that a small bug is usually better than a large one. Once, after he had caught five bass and I hadn't caught any, he threw me one of his small bugs and insisted that I use it. I began catching bass, too.

I remember the first time I ever fished with Claibourne. He took along his portable stove to cook our lunch on the bank, insisting that we didn't need to buy a main course — we would catch it.

That's confidence, I thought. And indeed, we had a good lunch of fish that day — all caught on Claibourne's fly rod. I fished with Claibourne many times after that, and there were few trips when he didn't catch enough fish for lunch.

James A. King Sr., a veteran fly rodder, said he thought one reason a bass bug is so deadly is that a bass will hit it even when he's not hungry or isn't in the mood to strike anything else. "The bass bug is so small, it's kind of like an hors d'oeuvre to him," Mr. King said.

Aubrey Edwards, another long-time fly rodder, agreed with his friend Jim King. "I remember once when Jim caught a nice bass on a popping bug, and we put the bass in the live well," Mr. Edwards recalled. "The bass spat out a large white perch. The perch was so big the bass couldn't possibly have been hungry when he hit Jim's bug."

One bass I caught on a fly rod on a Currituck trip confirmed Mr. King's theory. The water was so low and the aquatic grass so thick it looked as if you could walk on the water.

Wallace O'Neal, my friend and fishing guide, poled his skiff to within approximately 30 feet of a hole in the grass. The hole looked about the size of a Volkswagen Beetle. My partner, Curtis Youngblood, flipped the bail on his spinning reel and sent his Jitterbug sailing to the left side of the hole. I dropped my home-made popping bug — a bug just a little larger than a pencil eraser — to the opposite side of the hole, about 12 feet away from Curtis's Jitterbug.

Suddenly, the grass next to Curtis's lure quivered. A bass ran out, leaving a V-shaped wake. The bass almost accidentally bumped into the Jitterbug in its rush to get to my little bug way on the other side of the hole.

"Look at him coming!" I yelled. "Look at him coming!"

We watched as the bass ignored the Jitterbug and raced to my bug, which he clobbered. Curtis, who is usually mild-mannered, slammed his spinning rod on the boat seat so hard it's a wonder it didn't shatter.

"Darn!" he said. (At least, that's what I think he said.)

The bass was only about 13 inches long. But I had as much fun catching it as any other bass I ever caught.

Mr. King said a bass strikes a bug as soon as it lands on the water when there's another bass around. The bass grabs the bug quickly to prevent the other bass from getting it.

"If you'll throw right back to the same spot," Mr. King said, "you'll almost always catch another bass."

Dr. Baxter Caldwell, the dentist who uses a fly rod more than any other kind of tackle, said he believed one reason the fly rod often outfishes anything else is that it covers more water. "I'm not an expert with a fly rod," Baxter said, modestly. "But I have a friend who is the best I have ever seen with a spinning rod, and I outfish him nine times out of ten. An average fly rodder will catch more fish most of the time than an expert using a spinning rod or a casting rod."

The popping bug is ideal for fishing grass-infested waters. A popping bug is light and will often crawl over weeds without snagging. Also, you can make a cast to a hole in the grass, work out the hole with your bug, then lift the bug out and cast to another hole without ever touching the grass. With a spinning or casting outfit, you have to retrieve your lure all the way before you can make another cast.

There is no doubt that casting and spinning tackle will usually catch larger bass than a fly rod. But sometimes a fly rod will take a monster bass. Claibourne Darden has a ten-pound bass on his wall at home that he caught while fishing Currituck Sound with a fly rod. It may be the second-biggest bass ever caught on the sound on a fly rod, and it is one of the largest bass ever caught on the sound on any kind of tackle.

I once fished Currituck Sound with Andrew "Drew" Lewis, who later became secretary of transportation under President Reagan. He was so impressed with how well the fly rod performed that he later took a fly-fishing course.

Greensboro attorney Sidney Stern and his wife both took the Orvis fly-fishing course. Sidney said the course was worth the price from the standpoint of the enjoyable surroundings alone.

Of course, you don't need to take a course to learn a fly rod. Just find somebody like Roger Soles, Claibourne Darden, or Bodie McDowell.

You can get into fly fishing for a relatively modest outlay of money. I caught my first bass on an old yellow fly rod and a plastic reel that I bought for only about $10. I still use that old fiberglass rod occasionally. After you get hooked on the fly rod, however, you'll want to buy a bass-bug line, which will cost you about as much as the average fly reel. The line is one of the most important parts of your outfit. In fly fishing, it is the line that takes your bait out. In other kinds of fishing, the lure pulls the line out.

You can skimp on a reel. In bass fishing, it is the least impor-

tant part of your gear. It is basically a storage place for your line.
You land the fish by stripping the line in with your hands rather
than reeling the fish in.

Roger Soles once broke the foot of his reel while he was
fishing, and the reel wouldn't stay on the rod. He simply stripped
out line and continued to fish with the reel lying in the bottom of
the boat. He caught fish, too.

If you become as addicted to fly fishing for bass as I am, you'll
eventually want to replace your fiberglass rod with one made of
graphite. Hargrove "Skipper" Bowles, one of the state's best-
known sportsmen, owned the first graphite rod I ever used. He
urged us to try it out on the pier of the hunting and fishing lodge
where we were staying on Currituck Sound. In those days, graphite
rods were so expensive that we hesitated. Skipper insisted, and
several of us took turns casting it. After several casts, I could throw
a bug at least 25 percent farther than I could with my glass rod.
Hubert Breeze caught a bass on his first cast with the graphite rod.

Skipper, being the nice man he was, took great pleasure in that.
Sadly, our friend Skipper died a few years later. He was buried in
his favorite fishing outfit.

Graphite makes more difference in fly fishing than in any other
type of fishing. Graphite is not only light; it has an action that
makes for good casting. Another good friend, John Ellison, bought
one of the early graphite rods. His casting improved greatly, and he
is now very skilled with the fly rod. Fortunately, the price of
graphite rods has declined over the years to about what glass rods
once cost.

A fly rod will almost always take swirling bass. If you cast to a
swirl and don't get a hit, you can almost be sure it was not a bass
you saw. Also, you can usually tease a bass into hitting a popping
bug. Sometimes I've seen a bass swirl at my bug a half-dozen
times before nailing it.

But the best thing about using a fly rod is that it's the most
sporting way to catch bass. And that, after all, is what it's all about.

The
Pond Behind
The P.O.

—————————————————— Chapter 20

The Preacher And The Farm Ponds

Tired of trying to fish while dodging boaters and water skiers? How would you like to fish all day long and not be bothered by a single person? You can do it within a few miles of your home, even if you live in the middle of Durham, Raleigh, Greensboro, Charlotte, or some other North Carolina city. Furthermore, you stand a good chance of catching a bass so big it could make the outdoors pages of your local newspaper.

If you'd like to sample this kind of fishing, you should seek the advice of somebody like the Reverend Sam Sox. Reverend Sam became known far and wide — thanks to *Greensboro News & Record* outdoor writer Bodie McDowell — as "The Preacher Who Catches Bass in the Little Pond Behind the Post Office."

After Bodie started writing about Reverend Sam, the good reverend told me and everybody else who would listen that the "little pond behind the post office" was a synonym for "farm pond." Over the years, Reverend Sam developed into one of the state's top authorities on that type of fishing.

As North Carolina becomes more and more urbanized, farm pond fishing makes more and more sense, especially for the angler who likes to get away from the roar of the ski boat and the smell of gasoline fumes, and quietly contemplate the meaning of life.

Reverend Sam began fishing farm ponds in 1942 when he moved from his native Catawba County to Greensboro to accept a call from a large Lutheran church. "I really started farm pond fishing almost out of necessity," he recalled many years later. "I cut my eye teeth fishing on Lake Hickory, Lake James, and several smaller lakes that were built to provide power for cotton mill operations. One of the things I hated about moving to Greensboro was that, with my very limited financial resources, it would be impossible for me to go back to Lake Hickory and Lake James with any degree of regularity."

He first learned about the almost unlimited possibilities of farm pond fishing through a friend whose father owned one of the oldest man-made farm ponds in the state. The friend invited Reverend Sam to fish in the pond. The fishing was so good that it changed Reverend Sam's life. He became a true convert to farm-pond fishing. "I learned that in fishing a farm pond, you could catch fish and have just as much sport as you could on a large body of water."

Not too long after Reverend Sam's discovery of farm-pond fishing, something happened that was to enhance his reputation as an outdoorsman. While 'possum hunting one night, he fell out of a tree and injured his back. Despite the injury, he continued to fulfill his ministerial duties, even delivering his sermons from a bed by way of a remote hookup with his church.

The Greensboro paper caught wind of this and published a picture of him preaching from his sickbed. As a result of the publicity, Reverend Sam received many invitations to fish other farm ponds in Guilford County after he recovered from his injury.

But it was later that he became known as "The Preacher Who Catches Bass in the Pond Behind the Post Office." That happened after he caught a farm-pond bass that weighed more than nine pounds. He was so proud — who could blame him? — that he and his fishing companion carried the bass all over town to show it off. Bobby Andrew was the salesperson on duty in the fishing tackle department of Phipps Hardware when Reverend Sam and his friend arrived there with the bass.

Bobby asked the natural question: "Where did you catch it?"

Now, one of the first rules of farm-pond fishing is that you don't broadcast the location of a pond you have fished. That is an open invitation to poachers. Bobby, of course, didn't know that Reverend Sam had caught the bass in a private pond. As a good fisherman himself, Bobby wouldn't even have asked the question had he known the circumstances.

When the minister — trying neither to reveal his secret nor tell a falsehood — began mumbling, Bobby guessed the truth. So he tactfully answered his own question. "Oh," he said, "you caught him in the little pond behind the post office, did you?"

The next column Bodie McDowell wrote for the *Greensboro News & Record* contained a reference to the conversation between Bobby Andrew and Reverend Sam. After that, Reverend Sam caught many more big bass. Each time, Bodie duly recorded that the minister had caught the bass in the little pond behind the post office.

Some people took the joke seriously, especially after seeing pictures in the paper of the many huge bass caught by Reverend Sam. A few readers actually went in search of the pond. After all, the prospect of finding a fishing spot that holds such big bass has driven otherwise rational men to do even stranger things.

Once, somebody called Bodie and declared, "I've got it figured out where that preacher catches all those big bass. There's a pond not too far from the McLeansville Post Office." (McLeansville is a small, unincorporated community just east of Greensboro.)

Another caller to the *Greensboro News & Record* Sports Department complained, "I've lived in Greensboro all my life, and if there's a pond behind the post office, I don't know anything about it!" (The Greensboro Post Office is downtown in the city.)

After he caught that first big bass, Reverend Sam fished many other "ponds behind the post office" in different North Carolina counties. Out of this experience came some excellent ideas about how to get invitations to fish farm ponds — and how to get invited back after you've fished them the first time.

Some books on bass fishing suggest that one way to get permission to fish a pond is to just march up to a farm house, knock on the door, and ask the farmer. Reverend Sam said this might work on a rare occasion. But in this day and age, he asked, would you let a perfect stranger fish your pond?

"The best way is to know the owner or to know somebody who does know him," Reverend Sam said.

He observed that almost every angler knows at least one person who either owns a farm pond or knows somebody who knows somebody who owns a pond. Once you become known as a person who does not abuse the privilege of fishing a pond, you will get additional invitations, Reverend Sam declared.

Reverend Sam said a considerate farm-pond angler will observe these rules:

1. Never fish a farm pond unless you're invited to fish it.

2. Even if you have a standing invitation to fish a farm pond, never go to the pond unless the owner knows you're going.

3. Treat the pond as if it were your own. Don't litter or otherwise damage the pond.

4. When you fish a pond, don't overdo it. If you get a good catch, resist the temptation to go back the next day and the day after that. Otherwise, you'll make the owner feel like you're trying to "dry-clean" his pond — and you *can* dry-clean a farm pond.

5. If you think the owner of the farm pond likes to eat fish, offer him some of your catch.

By following these simple rules and being generally considerate, Reverend Sam made many friends among farm pond owners. "I have never fished a pond that I have not been invited back to," he said with some satisfaction.

Reverend Sam continued to practice what he preached after he retired from the active ministry — not only in fishing, but also in the rest of his life. His sense of humor made him many friends among both believers and nonbelievers. "People have asked me, 'Preacher, do you ever pray that the fish will bite?' I say, 'No, but I have asked the Good Lord to help me land a few that I knew were big ones.'"

Reverend Sam was quick to point out that fishing a farm pond requires skill. "It's a false statement that fishing a farm pond is like fishing in a washtub. The same skill you use in fishing big water is required in fishing farm ponds."

Long before he began fishing ponds, Reverend Sam was known as a good angler who could hold his own in big water.

In fishing a pond, he employed the same techniques and
principles he used on any other kind of water. For example, he used
surface lures in the spring, medium-running plugs later on, and so
forth. But he said his favorite lure for farm pond fishing — and
most other fishing, for that matter — was the Number 3 bronze
Mepps spinner with a piece of pork rind on the hook.

"It may be because I use it more consistently," he said. "But
that lure has produced more fish and bigger fish than any other lure
I've ever used."

He used the Mepps all year, but added, "It's particularly good
in, say, March, April, and May, and in September, October, and
November."

Reverend Sam nodded toward a 10-pound, 2-ounce largemouth
bass hanging on the wall of his study. "I caught that on a Mepps,"
he said.

"If you take any large lake and cut off a cove of it, you'd have
a farm pond — in the sense that what you find in a farm pond,
you'll also find in that particular cove. There are areas where you'll
find bream. There are areas where you'll find smaller bass. There
are areas where you'll find big bass."

He said his many years of fishing farm ponds convinced him
that in ponds, as in other types of water, there are areas that will
hold big bass year after year. In other words, you should remember
where you catch a big bass and fish it again, because you're likely
to catch other big bass in the same place.

He cited an example. In an area of about 75 square feet in one
farm pond — a pond so old that the original dam was constructed
with slave labor — he caught the following bass over several years:
a ten-pounder, a seven-pounder, and a six-pounder. And that pond,
large for a private pond, had been heavily fished over the years.

Reverend Sam discovered that a farm pond has another thing in
common with large water: No matter how good the pond might be,
the bass only strike on some days.

Still, he said, "You perhaps more consistently catch large bass
in a farm pond because you have a more confined area to fish in,
and the bass are seeing your bait more often if you throw it pretty
frequently. But it has been my experience that the same thing that

triggers a bass to strike — whatever that might be — in large bodies of water also triggers a bass to strike in farm ponds. If a bass is not ready to bite, he's not going to bite. I don't care if you throw a lure, or different lures, over him two dozen times, he's not going to strike whether he's in a farm pond or a larger body of water."

There is also some validity to the theory that bass grow larger in farm ponds because the private ponds are not as heavily fished as public water, Reverend Sam added.

But fishing in a farm pond can be just as unpredictable as fishing in any other type of water. He mentioned, for example, a lake he had fished many times without catching one large bass. "I went out one afternoon to that lake when the sky was overcast, and it looked like it was going to rain any minute. I put on a topwater crippled-minnow type of lure. I was still dubious about fishing on that particular afternoon. But on about the second cast, I twitched the lure about twice, and *Bam!* He caught me napping and I didn't set the hook.

"But before that afternoon was over, I caught six bass that weighed 16 pounds, and I lost two that I know would have gone as much or more than any I caught."

Reverend Sam recalled another day of great fishing when conditions were far from ideal. He and Dave Goforth — Dave is one of North Carolina's best all-around anglers — started out fishing for crappie on a private lake. "It was February," Reverend Sam said. "A northwest wind was blowing, and it was cold. I'm talking about really cold."

The crappie fishing, like the weather, was not good. So he and Dave, both of whom were beginning to get chills, decided to quit and return to the warmth of their homes. When Reverend Sam got out of the boat, he was numb.

"Dave," he said, "I'm going to walk down this bank and throw a few times to get the stiffness out."

Reverend Sam, of course, had a Mepps lure on his line. He cast about a half-dozen times. Then something happened that warmed his heart and body. He caught a three-pound bass.

Even though it was years later when he recalled that day, his face still lit up. "I went on a little farther and caught one that weighed four pounds. I hollered to Dave, who was putting his tackle up. I thought he was going to turn the car upside down getting his tackle back together."

Reverend Sam paused, reached into his desk drawer, and pulled out a photograph of he and Dave looking at a string of beautiful bass. "That very picture is a part of the string we caught that day. And we caught those fish in about 30 minutes. I believe to my soul we could have just dry-cleaned that farm pond if we had kept on fishing. That string of fish doesn't look like it, but it weighed 25 pounds."

Although the day he and Dave caught those fish was bitter cold, the week before had been warm. Reverend Sam noted that this happens during the winter just about every year in North Carolina.

"It can come as early as January," he said. "It can come in February. Or it can come as late as the first of March. But usually, you have a warm week in January or February. If you'll go out following that warm week at the tail end of it, the old boys will be on the bed."

This comment was almost identical to one made by Regis Dandar about fishing on the Pasquotank River, a river so huge that most farm ponds are like teacups in comparison. (See Chapter 4.)

Although Reverend Sam sometimes fishes farm ponds from a boat, he prefers fishing from the bank when possible. "It requires you to be a little stealthy," he said. "You've got to be quiet. You've got to creep around. Even the crack of a little twig may alarm the fish. But just the idea of trying to make yourself a part of the background of the area in which you are fishing fascinates me."

This requires more skill than fishing from a boat. The very spot where you sometimes find the most fish is sometimes the most difficult place to fish because of overhanging bushes or other obstructions. You have to make sidearm or underarm casts, or other types of casts you aren't often forced to make when fishing from a boat.

But Reverend Sam said it wasn't just the challenge that appealed to him about fishing from the bank. He said it is often easier to read the water from the bank than from a boat.

He also said that, while he knew many people disagreed with him, he thought it was easier to handle a big fish from the bank than from a boat.

He seldom used artificial worms, because he didn't enjoy them. They can, of course, be one of the most effective baits for farm-pond fishing, as elsewhere, in the hands of somebody who does enjoy using them.

Reverend Sam said there was something about farm-pond fishing that he liked even more than catching fish. "One of the things that makes farm-pond fishing so wonderful is that you learn to know the man who owns the pond. You go by and you talk with him awhile before you go fishing. And, in this way, you not only fish on that particular afternoon, but two personalities meet. And in the relaxed atmosphere, something takes place that nothing else will ever take the place of."

For the same reason, he enjoyed fishing with a friend. "I like to catch fish as much as anybody," he said. "But when I go fishing and have a buddy with me, I don't fish competitively."

Reverend Sam, like many people who love the outdoors, said he thought it was possible for a person to commune with nature. "I have a theory that man can attune himself to the out-of-doors to the point where he can sense the presence of fish, and whether he's going to catch them or not. He can go enough times that if he is conscious of how the general outdoors is at a particular time, he would bet his bottom dollar he would catch fish that particular afternoon. I think the whole secret is to go out there and be quiet so that you can actually become a part of the laws of nature, to the degree that you sense what is going on around you. If I had not had this experience repeated over and over again, I would not hold to that theory. But I have gone out, and I've thrown a lure at a certain place, and I would bet everything I own that I was going to catch a fish, and I did."

He added, "However, I've gone out when I had so many problems relative to my work that I didn't have the feeling, and nine times out of ten, I would not catch any fish. But if I had a particular feeling — I don't know how to explain it, other than I just seem to become a part of the out-of-doors, and was sensitive to everything around me, and appreciative of it — then I have caught fish. I believe that."

Reverend Sam paused for a long time. Then he said, "Another thing — and I say this without being overly pious, because you know me and know that I am not — I know that you can go fishing and be unconscious of the Great God who made the out-of-doors, and still catch fish. But if you are conscious of His presence and feel He is there with you, the day is far more enjoyable."

Trolling

Chapter 21

It's Not Just Dragging A Lure

If you are like most anglers, your favorite way to fish is with topwater lures. Your next favorite way to fish is casting in shallow water. If that is unsuccessful, you will settle for casting or jigging in deep water.

But there is still another way, often a very effective way, of fishing for bass: trolling. Trolling for bass is now almost a lost art. But it is ideally suited for North Carolina's man-made reservoirs.

Some otherwise good anglers look down their noses at trolling; they think it is a lazy way of fishing. L.E. "Buck" Perry of Hickory, perhaps the country's most knowledgeable fresh-water angler, disagreed.

"Trolling — when it's done right — is one of the most difficult things there is to fishing," Buck declared. "There's a difference between trolling and dragging a lure through the water."

Buck, sometimes known as the "father of modern structure fishing," coined the word *structure* as it applies to fishing. That was many years ago, before most of today's tournament anglers were even old enough to lift a rod and reel. Buck, in fact, concocted the vocabulary — consisting of words such as *breaks* and *breaklines* — that later became common to describe structure fishing.

Buck's theories have long since proven to be more than mere theories. They are practical. During his fishing seminars, he caught fish after fish with hundreds of people looking on.

Buck was the subject of many articles in metropolitan newspapers from New York to San Francisco, written by reporters and outdoor writers who personally witnessed his amazing ability to find and catch fish. He was also the subject of outdoor movies, and he appeared on national radio and television shows. And his writing — books, pamphlets, and magazine articles — could fill a small library.

When Buck first evolved his method of intermixing trolling and casting to catch fish, there were no lures on the market that would do exactly what he wanted. So Buck, a former college physics professor, used his knowledge of physics to develop — after many days on the water with tools and pieces of metal — a lure he named the Spoonplug. That lure is probably the best trolling lure ever invented to date. It is a good casting lure, too.

"I had to have a tool that would allow me to map the bottom, to tell me what was down there," he recalled. "I had to have a lure that could walk on the bottom. I had to have one that would sink and that would maintain its depth, regardless of the speed."

Buck invented the Spoonplug to give him control of speed and depth for both trolling and casting. *Control of depth and speed —* that was a term he used over and over again while discussing "Spoonplugging."

But Buck didn't claim that the Spoonplug was the only lure good for trolling. Many other lures, however, will flip out of the water when trolled fast. The Spoonplug is a sinking metal lure and quickly gets to its assigned depth. The depth depends on the size of the spoon plug, the size of the line, and the speed at which the Spoonplug is trolled. The Spoonplug also sheds weeds more easily when you give it a hard jerk.

Buck once told me that he almost always trolled until he located fish. Then he went back and cast. Using this method, he located some unbelievable schools of big bass.

"Trolling will tell you how, when, where, and what to cast," he explained. "If you just tie on a lure and haphazardly cast, you're just wishing. The guy who catches the most fish is the guy who is making the most casts. Trolling is a teacher."

Despite his expertise in trolling, he believed he caught more bass casting than he did trolling. Still, he added, he always started off a fishing trip by trolling.

"Trolling tells me something about the lake, even if I don't catch a fish," he declared. "But 90 percent of the time, if he's there, I'll catch him."

He said that if an angler learned how to interpret the water, the weather, and the features on the lake bottom, successful fishing boiled down to a machine-like process.

Buck also pioneered the study of the movement of fish along structure, breaks, and breaklines. He contended that anglers who learned how structure and other factors affected the movement of fish should be able to catch fish under nearly all conditions.

"Then catching fish becomes even further a mechanical process of controlling the depth and speed of your lures," he said. "This control of your depth and speed is done by two main methods of fishing: casting and trolling. One is no more important than the other. In order to become a good fisherman and get to the point where you always get better and better and better, you must use both methods of presentation. Sometimes, one will work. Sometimes, the other will work."

There are several rules of thumb for trolling, Buck said.

"First, you learn how to troll the shallow water. Every time you catch a fish, you go back and cast." Shallow water, Buck said, is anything from zero to eight or ten feet.

"The next thing you do is learn how to troll deep water. Every time you catch a fish, you go back and cast. You do it exactly the same way every time. There will be no strange water ever existing. In one day's time, you'll learn more about a lake than they guy who has been living there 30 years."

He advocated trolling in a triangle. That way, he said, you can "strain" the water.

Buck divides lures into three categories:

1. *Topwater and shallow-running lures.* These lures have little value in the method of fishing he developed.

2. *The free-running, bottom-bumping lure.* The Spoonplug is this type of lure, as are the Hellbenders, Water Dogs, Bombers, and the like.

3. *Jump lures.* These include lures that lack any action of their own: jigs, weighted plastic worms, and spoons, such as the Hopkins. The angler must impart the action.

Buck said that in some instances, he continued to use the Spoonplug when going back to cast after catching a fish trolling. At other times, he said, he switched to a jump lure — especially if he caught the fish in deep water.

"I jump it and let it go back to the bottom," he said of the jump lure. "I take up my slack as it is going to the bottom."

Buck was among the first to use high speeds in fishing — both in casting and in trolling. Until he proved otherwise, most anglers believed that freshwater bass were not fast enough to catch up with a swiftly moving lure. "Normally, as the temperature goes up, you increase your speed," he said. "As the temperature goes down, you decrease your speed."

Buck advised retrieving or trolling the fastest in warm, shallow water. That's where the Spoonplug comes in handy. Most other lures won't maintain their depths and action when you troll fast.

He said he slowed down the speed of his fishing as the water got cooler, or as he increased the depth of his fishing. Long before anglers began using electronic depth finders, Buck used his lures as "depth finders." He mapped the bottoms of lakes by feeling the signals the lures sent to him as he trolled.

He also was one of the first to recognize that deep water is where bass spend most of their time. Although bass periodically move to shallow water, he discovered that they move back to deep water to make their "homes." It is when the fish are in deep water that people complain "They are just not biting" as an excuse for not catching fish.

"It's not that they aren't biting," he said. "It's that you are fishing where the fish aren't. If you can train people to fish down to 30 to 35 feet, there will be very few times when they will come off the lake without fish."

Over the years, Buck also discovered that when you catch fish in one place on a lake during a day, you will most likely catch other fish in similar places elsewhere on the lake that day.

So mark down another first for Buck Perry. Modern-day anglers call that "pattern fishing."

Trolling was once a popular way of fishing for bass. Buck said he thought the popularity of trolling declined in almost exact proportion to the rise of the modern bass boat. "You just can't troll efficiently with a bass boat," he declared.

And it's not all a matter of speed; a bass boat can be equipped with a plate that will cut down on its speed. "It's a matter of maneuverability," Buck explained. A bass boat can't turn as quickly as a smaller boat.

For trolling, Buck said he didn't like stick or wheel steering, or boats with engines more powerful than ten horsepower. Another reason bass boats are not good for trolling, he said, is that most have long-shank motors, making them unsuitable for trolling in shallow water.

Buck developed special equipment for trolling: a short, stiff rod and a light, direct-drive "service reel" that has a star drag and anti-reverse. He also developed a line that has the stretch removed and is marked so you know how much line you have out when you catch a fish.

I remember reading a *Charlotte Observer* story about a day of fishing that Buck and former Governor Luther Hodges enjoyed while using Buck's methods. They caught fish after fish on a day when most people weren't catching anything.

On another occasion, Buck caught 33 bass on 33 consecutive casts. That was during a seminar when nearly 300 people were watching. He once caught 49 fish on 49 consecutive casts, too. On still another day, he caught 10 bass that weighed a total of 89 pounds. An angler who becomes adept at Buck's methods stands a better-than-average chance of catching a lunker.

Buck's wife, "Bud," a remarkable woman, became a "Spoon-plugger" in her own right. She often caught fish when everybody else was complaining that "the fish just aren't biting."

For more information on Buck's methods, write:

Buck's Baits
P.O. Box 66
Hickory, N.C. 28601

I caught my first bass while trolling on Lake Murray, South Carolina. I also caught my largest bass to date, one that weighed 9 pounds 14 ounces, while trolling. I was only about nine years old when I caught that big bass. I was fishing with my dad and one of his fishing friends, Roscoe "Sweeney" Kennington of Rock Hill, South Carolina.

In those days we did exactly the opposite of what Buck Perry suggested. We switched to trolling only if we had no luck casting; we thought casting was more sporting.

One fishing experience I will always remember is something that happened to Dad and me while we were trolling. Dad pointed ahead of the boat and said, "What is that?"

It was a big patch of pink water. We passed through the pink slick and our lures ran under it.

"I've got one," I yelled.

"I have, too," Dad said as he shut down the motor.

I reeled in a small bass and removed the fish from the black-and-white Heddon's Go-Deeper lure I was using. Dad had difficulty landing what we assumed was a large bass that had struck his yellow Flat Fish.

Finally, Dad got the fish up to the side of the boat. It wasn't a bass. It was a gar that was almost as long as I was tall at the time. We made about a dozen other passes at the same spot. Each time, I caught a bass and Dad caught a gar.

We concluded that the gar and the bass were fighting because several of the bass had wounds. The pink spot was blood. That was when I first discovered how mean — and brave — a largemouth bass can be. The gar is a throwback to a prehistoric fish whose scales are almost as tough as armor. A bass has about as much of a chance against a gar as a motorcyclist against a Sherman tank. The gar also has a bill similar to a swordfish's. And its teeth can sever a person's fingers.

Hubert Greene of Lake Lure, the fine deep-water angler, agreed with Buck Perry that trolling is a good way to learn a new lake and an effective method of taking fish.

"In the early days, before we had depth finders," Hubert recalled, "we'd gain all of the knowledge about the bottom of lakes with our lures while were trolling."

Hubert said his favorite lure for trolling was a shallow-running Rapala. He first tried trolling with that lure with lead-core line as an experiment.

"I wanted to get a Rapala down deep," he said. "We know how good it is up here" — he motioned with his hand, indicating shallow water — "but it was even better down deep."

The experiment worked. Many times, Hubert said, the Rapala didn't have to run very far before a bass hit it.

Fishing In The Dark

Chapter 22

Getting Away From Traffic And The Summer Sun

Some people still think of North Carolina as one of the country's most rural states. Yet on holidays and summer weekends, many of our public lakes are so crowded, they look like Coney Island.

On a typical July weekend, you risk your life when you venture out on a lake. Water skiers churn the water; high-powered bass boats roar up and down; pleasure boaters whiz by, rocking smaller boats in their wakes. This frenzy erodes the banks and leaves a muddy ring around the shoreline.

Some anglers continue to fish — and to catch fish — in the middle of all this traffic. As Blake Honeycutt said, "I think water skiers bother the fisherman more than the fish."

True. But if you are like me, it takes a lot of the pleasure out of fishing.

So what do you do if the weekend is the only time you have to fish, and the only waters you have to fish are the public lakes in the populous Piedmont?

Cheer up. There is a way you can go fishing in the summer and avoid the multitudes, the hot-rodders, and even the blazing summer sun. Furthermore, you will often catch your limit of bass.

You can fish at night. It is an enjoyable, pleasant time to fish.

I remember the night I discovered how sensational night fishing can be. It happened almost as an afterthought.

A friend, Jack Bilyeu, and I fished a private lake about 15 miles from downtown Greensboro on a hot summer afternoon. Not only didn't we catch any fish all afternoon, it was so hot we were

afraid we'd become dehydrated. Jack suggested we stop fishing, go
to the clubhouse, and get some sandwiches and something cold to
drink.

When we finished eating, the sun was still high. We shot a few
games of pool to kill time.

"Have you ever done any night fishing?" Jack asked.

"Not much," I said, missing a shot.

"You want to try it tonight?" Jack asked.

We called our wives to tell them we'd be late, then shot a few
more games of pool, got a flashlight out of the car, and returned to
the lake. There was still a little light when we started fishing, and
we caught a few bass on Cordell Hot Spots.

Then the sun dipped from view entirely, leaving the night deep,
dark, and mysterious. We switched to black Jitterbugs, which we
had read were good lures to use at night. There was a full moon,
and it bathed the lake in a soft, misty glow. There were scattered
clouds in the sky, and every now and then one drifted across the
face of the moon. The stars seemed so close, you felt your rod
would brush against them when you made a cast. One star tumbled
from its orbit, trailing bright sparks across the heavens and scatter-
ing their reflections in the water beside our ancient wooden boat.

Somewhere off in the distance, an owl cried mournfully. Night
insects buzzed, and a whippoorwill whistled. Frogs bellowed
loudly. Fireflies left yellow streaks in the air. The water lapped
gently against the hull.

Jack and I were fishing near the Piedmont Triad International
Airport, off Interstate 40 between Greensboro and Winston-Salem,
but the only signs of civilization were the occasional jets that
roared overhead, their landing lights piercing the night sky.

The air seemed nice and cool compared to the withering
Southern heat of just two hours earlier.

Jack, sitting in the stern of the boat, cast his Jitterbug out into
the mist and darkness. The plop the lure made when it hit the water
was followed immediately by a thrashing sound, and Jack reeled in
a bass that weighed about three pounds.

The fishing was good. Sometimes the bass would hit as soon as
our Jitterbugs landed on the water. At other times, we would let our

lures sit still for a second or two, and the bass would hit before we started retrieving. On some casts, the bass would hit only after we started our retrieves.

Then a strange thing happened. When a cloud briefly obscured the moon, we got strikes on almost every cast. But as soon as the cloud moved on, leaving the moon free to throw its light onto the lake again, the bass didn't hit as well.

We caught a lot of bass. At about 3 a.m., more clouds formed, and Jack and I saw jagged streaks of lightning on the horizon and heard the distant growl of thunder. We thought we smelled rain in the air. We decided to quit fishing; we were getting sleepy anyway.

The black Jitterbug — the lure Jack and I used that night — has long been a popular lure for night fishing.

The Reverend Sam Sox, a Greensboro friend, began night fishing many years ago around Hickory, where he then lived. "I remember when the Jitterbug first came out," he recalled. "These two buddies of mine had Jitterbugs, and they told me a day before we were to go fishing, 'Get you a Jitterbug. They're eating it up.'

"We went up to Lake James and started fishing at just about dark, but to no avail. We usually had a lantern up in front of the boat so you could see the outline of the shore, and we fished until the moon came up. Fortunately, just as soon as the moon came up, we came to the side of an island where the moon was shining, and, buddy, for about 30 or 40 minutes, every time you'd throw to the bank, *Wham!*

"If one would miss it, another would hit it. I didn't have my Jitterbug on. I stuck my hand about a dozen times getting that Jitterbug on. Oh, boy!"

Night in and night out, black is the best color for a topwater lure. That seems strange, yet it is true. Apparently, the dark color presents a better silhouette against the night sky. Mark Twain once wrote that steamboat pilots could see black logs on the water at night much better than they could see white objects. A fish's vision must be at least as good as a steamboat pilot's.

I have also caught fish with the luminous Jitterbug at night. (You have to shine a light on the lure periodically to activate the paint and make it glow in the dark.) But I've had the best luck with a black lure.

Years ago, almost all night fishing was done with noisy topwater lures, principally the black Jitterbug. But in recent years, many good anglers have started using underwater lures at night.

The spinner bait is one of the most widely used lures for night fishing on the Linville River side of Lakes James. Anglers begin using it on Lake James in the spring, and continue using it right on through the summer.

Hubert Green, the good mountain lake angler, said his night fishing changed over the years. "It used to be that I would fish at night from about March on up. But I like night fishing, particularly in the summer months. When you go out there in the day, and bake all day long in the sun, you just don't feel good. Night fishing is just pleasant.

"We started out with topwater at night, and then we began to use crankbaits," Hubert said. "The last few years, we've got onto worm fishing at night, especially in crystal-clear lakes. The spinner bait is good at night, too. But we've had real good success with black worms and black grape worms at night, and we fish them now mostly.

"We fish points that during the day we can't produce a fish on — points on which there is all kinds of brush. We know they are there, but we just can't get them to hit. We go back at night to the same points, and they just eat us up."

So even when you are fishing underwater lures, such as artificial worms, you are likely to have your best luck on dark-colored lures.

Hubert said he continued to use topwater lures some at night. "But we just don't produce as many fish on top as we used to. It seems like black is best in topwater baits, but I also have a gray and white Jitterbug that is good at night."

Hubert said you should fish shallow water at night in hot weather more often than you fish it in the daytime. He theorized that fish stay deep during the day to escape boat traffic and other disturbances.

"But in real clear water at night, I sometimes fish as deep as from 10 to 15 feet," he said, explaining that these depths were still more shallow than he fished in the daytime under the same conditions. Hubert also said he used a larger artificial worm at night, and let this lure (or whatever lure he was using) hit the water harder than he did during the day. "That noise gets them."

As evidence that noise helps at night, Hubert recalled something that had happened to him many times. "You can fish a flat bottom all night and not catch a thing, and, all of a sudden, come across a little limb, and you'll feel your worm hit. Look out! He'll hit it right after it comes across the limb. You get his attention by that noise, although he might hit it after it comes across the limb and starts falling."

Many other experts agree that a little noise helps attract a bass to a lure at night. Some anglers even add rattle devices to their artificial worms.

Luther Turpin, the Fontana Lake dock manager, said a black Jitterbug is probably the best night lure for his part of the country. But he said he also fished big-lipped Rebels in the mouths of the rivers that flow into the lakes. These lures run deep and bang the bottom in the relatively shallow waters of the rivers, making noise to grab the attention of the bass.

This may also help explain why a spinner bait is often so attractive to bass at night. The whirling spinners produce sound.

If you've never been fishing at night and want to try it, here are a few rules that will help you:

— Be even more careful at night than you are during the day. Your visibility is limited, and it's easy to make a false step and tumble out of the boat.

— Even a familiar lake looks different at night. Try to remember where you are at all times.

— Despite the experience Jack Bilyeu and I had the night we fished the private lake, try to go fishing when there is at least some moonlight. You can see better, and the fish usually hit better when there is some light. Besides, I think it makes the fishing more pleasant. A lake is more beautiful in the moonlight than at any other time.

— Take two good flashlights along, keeping one as a spare in case you drop the first one overboard. But use your light as sparingly as possible. When you do have to use a light, shade it so that it doesn't shine out over the water. A wayward beam of light often spooks the fish. Another reason to use your light as little as possible: It takes your eyes a few minutes to adjust to the darkness after you douse the light.

— Arrange your tackle so you can change lures with a minimum of noise and light. While noise generated by a lure on the water may attract bass, a noise in a boat frightens them.

— Be careful when you change lures; it's easier to hook yourself when your vision is reduced. A snap swivel can make changing lures easier. Most lure manufacturers say a swivel inhibits the action of their lures, but the action isn't as critical at night as it is in the daytime. Another thing that will help you avoid fumbling around in the dark is to carry several fully-rigged outfits.

— Check the latest boating regulations and be sure you have the proper running lights for your boat. If you don't have them, get them.

Good night and good fishing.

In
Memoriam

Farewell To A Great Guide

(By Buck Paysour — reprinted from the *Greensboro News & Record*.)

AYDLETT — A quail whistled softly in the distance, and a snowy white egret flew overhead last Monday as Wallace O'Neal Jr. was laid to rest on a knoll overlooking his beloved Currituck Sound.

The weather was mild, and there was not a cloud in the deep blue sky. On the horizon, across the sound on the Outer Banks, the sun highlighted the sand dunes. The water on the sound was in one of its rare glass-calm moods.

It was as if all of Currituck had paused to pay tribute to the passing of one of its own and to mourn the end of an era.

O'Neal, 80, was the oldest active fishing guide on the vast and wild Currituck Sound. His friend and fellow guide, Ed Cartwright, had died just a few weeks before. Next to O'Neal, Cartwright had been the oldest.

O'Neal had guided through the past spring fishing season and was already making plans to guide during the fall season. During his long career, O'Neal had guided for some of the world's most famous anglers. Some of their names had graced the pages of outdoor magazines, and some had appeared on national television programs.

Others who stepped into his skiff came from all over the country to get a little relaxation and escape from pressure-filled lives.

They included bankers, doctors, lawyers, people prominent in politics, and chief executive officers of large corporations. They also included truck drivers, service station operators, and store clerks.

He treated them all alike. On the water, he was boss. Although he enjoyed a good joke as much as anyone, he would not tolerate foolishness that could be dangerous in his small skiff.

O'Neal was broad-minded, but he frowned on fishermen who overindulged in alcoholic beverages while fishing. He felt people should go fishing to fish and save the drinking for the hunting and fishing lodge at night.

He disliked excess in all things and would refuse to again guide for people who insisted on keeping more than their limits of fish.

Among serious sportsmen, there was not a more respected or popular guide on the sound.

O'Neal lived on Currituck Sound all his life, and most of his several careers were related to the sound. He had fished its depths, farmed its shores, trapped its marshes, and hunted on its waters.

Even when he was in the Coast Guard in the early 1900s, he never got very far away from his sound. He was stationed on the narrow spit of land that separates Currituck Sound from the ocean. It is part of what is known as the "Graveyard of the Atlantic" because of the numerous shipwrecks that have occurred there.

Surfboats were used by Coast Guardsmen then, and O'Neal recalled how both survivors and bodies were plucked off foundering ships.

"We used mules and wagons to take away the bodies," he said.

Especially on the east side, Currituck Sound is still one of the most unspoiled and remote spots in the state. An occasional eagle still soars overhead. Like the sound, O'Neal was unspoiled and completely honest. If, after a fishing trip, he found a beat-up 75-cent lure in his skiff, he would carefully wrap it and mail it back to its owner.

He was not a big man physically, but even in his latter years his arms bulged with muscles that would put younger men to shame. That was a result of hard work, including poling his skiff around the sound.

He would continue fishing long after the howling wind had driven many of the younger guides and their parties back to the comfort of the hunting and fishing lodges.

One of O'Neal's fishing friends once accidentally stuck him in the ear with a fishing hook. Although O'Neal wanted to remove the hook, it was in the flesh at an angle that would have made it difficult. So the friend insisted that O'Neal go to a doctor.

The waves on the open sound were five or six feet high when O'Neal finally consented to make the trip back across to the land side. He had to pull the plug in the bottom of his open skiff so that the water would run out and not swamp the boat. The spray hit the two fishermen and O'Neal in blinding sheets.

As the boat tossed and churned its way across the sound, one of the fishermen asked O'Neal, "Have you ever turned a boat over out here?"

"No," O'Neal replied, his voice calm despite the hook hanging from his ear and the strain of keeping the boat headed in the right direction. "And I don't intend to start now."

O'Neal guided for hunters during the duck season until a few years ago when the biting Currituck winters forced him to retire — about the only concession he ever made to advancing age.

Even as he approached his 80th birthday, O'Neal wore glasses only for reading, and he was still an excellent shot. He carried his shotgun slung under the seats of his skiff. Once, while guiding for a man and his wife from Greensboro, O'Neal pointed to a clump of marsh grass and said, "Look at the mallard hen. She's afraid that cottonmouth is going to get her chicks."

The fisherman and his wife had to strain to see the snake, but O'Neal was already unwrapping the gun. He reached into his pocket, took out a shell, loaded the gun, aimed, and shot.

He cut the snake's head off.

The mallard seemed to sense that the man making all that noise and belching fire and smoke was a friend. She didn't even flinch. O'Neal was on close speaking terms with nature itself.

Sometimes, when you were fishing with him on a cloudy day, he would suggest, "You might want to get your rain pants on so that all you'll have to do is put your jacket on when it rains. We're going to get a shower in a minute."

You would look up and wonder how he knew that. But a

shower would come, and very soon.

The rain would often be so hard that O'Neal would pull the boat next to the marsh so that you would have at least some shelter. Then, before there would be any visible sign to you that the rain was letting up, he would say, "Get ready to start fishing again. It's about to stop."

And it would.

A remarkable man in almost every way, it was obvious to people who knew him that O'Neal had an above-average I.Q. Largely a self-taught man, he was well-read and could converse intelligently and interestingly on a wide variety of subjects.

He was one of the few people on the sound who still hand-carved duck decoys out of wood. These are now so rare that they are becoming art objects. He made his own "shoving oars" — long poles used to push a boat over the sound. These required hours of patient work. They had to be flat at the end, so they wouldn't sink into the soft bottom of the sound, and smooth at the top, so they wouldn't blister the user's hands. O'Neal's oars were so good they were much in demand by other guides.

He made his own three-person fishing skiffs, too, and they were among the most seaworthy on the sound.

O'Neal lived a satisfying life, and this was well illustrated by a conversation O'Neal had with a successful young Pennsylvanian who fished with him not many years ago. It was a beautiful day, almost like the day the old guide was buried, except that fall had already arrived and the wild ducks and geese were flying overhead.

The Pennsylvanian — who was later to become the Republican nominee for governor of his state — asked O'Neal, "How long have you lived on this sound?"

"I've made a living on this sound all my life," O'Neal replied. Then he thought for a minute and added, "And you know, I believe if I had my whole life to live over, I wouldn't change much about it."

"That's the mark of a successful man," the young Pennsylvanian remarked, almost enviously.

Author's note: The young Pennsylvanian was Andrew "Drew" Lewis, who later served as secretary of transportation under President Ronald Reagan.

Appendix A

N.C. Wildlife Resources Commission Launching Areas

(The N.C. Wildlife Resources Commission adds ramps from time to time. For an up-to-date listing, contact the commission. Watch for distinctive signs giving directions to access areas.)

Alligator River
Dare County (East Lake Ferry): North side of the East Lake Bridge.
Tyrrell County (Gum Neck Landing): 20 miles south of Columbia via U.S. 94, State Roads 1321, 1320, and 1316.
Tyrrell County (Frying Pan): 12.5 miles southeast of Columbia near the end of State Road 1307.

Appalachia Lake
Cherokee County (Appalachia): Immediately downstream from the south side of Hiwassee Dam.

Badin Lake
Montgomery County (Beaver Dam): 14.5 miles south of Denton on State Road 2551.
Montgomery County (Lakemont): Turn off N.C. 109 on State Road 1156 at Blaine, then onto State Road 1158.

Bear Creek Lake
Jackson County (Bear Creek): 5.1 miles east of Tuckasegee off N.C. 281 on State Road 1137.

Big Flatty Creek
Pasquotank County (Big Flatty): From N.C. 168 at Weeksville, take State Road 1103 to State Road 1104 to State 1108, approximately 6 miles from Weeksville.

Big Swamp Creek
Robeson County (Lennons's Bridge): On State Road 1002, .3 miles from the Columbus County line.

Black River
Bladen County (Hunt's Bluff): 8 miles east of Kelly, south of N.C. 53 on State Road 1547.
Sampson County (Ivanhoe): Just south of Ivanhoe on State Road 1100.

Blewett Falls Lake
Anson County (Pee Dee): 2 miles north of the Pee Dee River Bridge (U.S. 74) via State Road 1748 and State Road 1747.
Richmond County (Grassy Island): 5 miles west of Ellerbe on State Road 1148.

Bogue Sound
Carteret County (Morehead City): On the east side of U.S. 70 near the western limits of Morehead City.

Brice's Creek
Craven County (Brice's Creek): In Croatan National Forest on the Forest Service continuation of State Road 1143.

Cape Fear River
Bladen County (Elwell's Ferry): 2 miles northeast of Carvers at Elwell's Ferry via State Road 1730.
Bladen County (Tar Heel): 1 mile northeast of N.C. 87 on State Road 1316.

Chatham County (Avent's Ferry Bridge): 2 miles southwest of Corinth via N.C. 42 at Avent's Ferry Bridge.
Cumberland County (Fayetteville): 4 miles south of Fayetteville on North Carolina 87.
Harnett County (Lillington): 3 miles east of Lillington via State Road 2016.

Cape Fear River Basin
New Hanover County (Federal Point): At the end of U.S. 421 in New Hanover County near Fort Fisher.

Cedar Cliff Lake
Jackson County: From N.C. 107 at Tuckasegee, take State Road 1135 east to the area.

Chatuge Lake
Clay County (Jack Rabbit): From U.S. 64, 4 miles east of Hayesville, take State Road 1154 2.5 miles south of State Road 1155, then 1.2 miles to the area.
Clay County (Ledford's Chapel): 5 miles east of Hayesville via U.S. 64 and State Road 1151.

Cheoah Lake
Graham County (Cheoah): Adjacent to N.C. 28.

Chowan River
Chowan County (Cannon's Ferry): 13 miles north of Edenton on N.C. 32, turn left on State Road 1231. Go 1 mile to the area.
Chowan County (Edenhouse Bridge): Adjacent to U.S. 17.
Gates County (Gatesville): 3 miles from the Gates County Courthouse on State Road 1111.
Hertford County (Tunis): From N.C. 45 at Colfield, take State Road 1403 to State Road 1400 to State Road 1402, then go .8 miles to the area.

Conaby Creek
Washington County (Conaby Creek): On N.C. 45 approximately 3 miles north of U.S. 64.

Contentnea Creek
Greene County (Snow Hill): At Snow Hill, 1 block east of U.S. 258.
Pitt County (Grifton): In town limits of Grifton on Contentnea Creek.

Currituck Sound
Currituck County (Poplar Branch): At end of N.C. 3, .7 miles off U.S. 158 north of Grandy.

Dan River
Caswell County (Milton): Just northwest of Milton on N.C. 62.
Rockingham County (Leaksville): N.C. 14, 1 mile from Leaksville.

Dawson Creek
Pamlico County (Dawson Creek): Off State Road 1302, 4 miles southwest of Oriental.

Deep River
Moore County (Carbonton): Just south of Carbonton on State Road 1621.
Randolph County (Sandy Creek): .5 miles west of Ramseur of U.S. 64.

East Lake
Dare County (Mashoes): 3 miles north of Manns Harbor on State Road 1113.

Falls of the Neuse Lake

Durham County (Hickory Hill): At intersection of Interstate 85 and State Road 1632 just east of Durham, exit onto State Road 1632 south to State Road 1670. Go east on State Road 1670 to State Road 1637 to the area.

Wake County (Ledge Rock): Travel from Raleigh north to State Road 1901, west on State Road 1901 to the intersection of State Road 1903, south on State Road 1903 to the intersection of State Road 1725, east on State Road 1725 to the area.

Wake County (Upper Barton's Creek): Travel from Raleigh north on N.C. 50 to junction of N.C. 98, go approximately 1.5 miles to junction of State Road 1005, then south approximately 1 mile. The area is on the left.

Fontana Lake

Graham County (Cable Cove): About 5 miles east of Fontana Village on N.C. 28 to the U.S. Forest Service Cable Cove campground.

Swain County (Flat Branch): From Bryson City, follow U.S. 19 west to State Road 1320, right to State Road 1311, right to State Road 1312, left to State Road 1313 and the area.

Swain County (Tsali): From N.C. 18 at the Graham-Swain county line, take the Forest Service Road north to the area.

Gaston Lake

Halifax County (Summit): East of Littleton, 1 mile north of U.S. 158 on State Road 1458.

Northhampton County (Henrico): From N.C. 46 on State Road 1214, 6.5 miles west to the area.

Warren County (Stonehouse Creek): 3.5 miles north of Littleton on State Road 1357.

Glenville Lake
Jackson County (Lake Thorpe): From Cullowhee, travel N.C. 107 approximately 15 miles south to State Road 1157 and turn right. The area is 2.8 miles on the left.

Hancock Creek
Craven County (Hancock Creek): From Havelock go east on N.C. 101, 3.5 miles, then 2.2 miles on State Road 1717.

Hickory Lake
Alexander County (Steel Bridge): 2 miles north of Hickory on N.C. 127 to State Road 1208, to State Road 1141 to the area.
Alexander County (Dusty Ridge): From Interstate 40, travel N.C. 16 north 8.5 miles to State Road 1135, left on State Road 1135 1.2 miles to State Road 1137, left on State Road 1137 2.3 miles to State Road 1138, left on State Road 1138 .6 miles to State Road 1185, right on State Road 1185 .2 miles to the area.
Caldwell County (Gunpowder): On U.S. 321 north, .4 miles north of Catawba River Bridge, turn east on Grace Chapel Road (State Road 1758), 3 miles to State Road 1757, turn north 1.3 miles to the area.
Caldwell County (Lovelady): On U.S. 321 north, .4 miles north of the Catawba River Bridge, turn east on Grace Chapel Road (State Road 1758) 3 miles to State Road 1757, turn south .9 miles to the area.
Catawba County (Oxford): Southwest of Oxford Dam via N.C. 16 and State Road 1453 to Lake Hickory Campground Road, 1.2 miles to the area.

High Rock Lake
Rowan County (Dutch Second Creek): 8 miles southeast of Salisbury at Bringle's Ferry Road Bridge (State Road 1002).

Hiwassee Lake
Cherokee County (Grape Creek): 5 miles northwest of Murphy on Joe Brown Highway (State Road 1326).
Cherokee County (Hanging Dog): From Murphy, take State Road 1326 approximately 3 miles northwest to the area.

Intracoastal Waterway
Brunswick County (Oak Island): From Southport take N.C. 211 west to N.C. 133, follow N.C. 133 south to State Road 1101, turn left, and the area is .5 miles on the left.
Brunswick County (Sunset Harbor): At the junction of U.S. 17 and N.C. 211 near Supply, travel southeast on N.C. 211 approximately 7 miles to the junction of N.C. 211 and State Road 1112. Follow State Road 1112 south to the access area.
Carteret County (Cedar Point): 1 mile north of Swansboro on N.C. 24.
Currituck County (Coinjock): 1 mile east of Coinjock on State Road 1142.
New Hanover County (Snow's Cut): Near Carolina Beach, 1 mile east of U.S. 421 at the south end of the bridge.
New Hanover County (Wrightsville Beach): Adjacent to the U.S. 74-76 drawbridge on the Intracoastal Waterway.
Onslow County (Turkey Creek): From Folkstone on U.S. 17, turn northeast on State Road 1518, approximately 3 miles to State Road 1529, turn east on State Road 1529, approximately 2 miles to State Road 1530, and proceed south on State Road 1530 approximately 1 mile to the area.
Onslow County (West Onslow Beach): At the intersection of U.S. 17 and N.C. 210 near Dixon, travel east on N.C. 210 approximately 10 miles. The area is on the northeast side of the Intracoastal Waterway bridge.

James Lake

Burke County (Canal Bridge): 2 miles northwest of Bridgewater on N.C. 126.

Burke County (Linville River): 1 mile east of Linville River Bridge on N.C. 126.

McDowell County (Hidden Cove): On N.C. 126 approximately .5 miles south of the Catawba Spillway.

McDowell County (North Fork): .5 miles north of the U.S. 221-70 intersection west of Marion via State Road 1501 and 1552.

Jordan Lake

Chatham County (Farrington Point): From the intersection of U.S. 64 and State Road 1008 in Chatham County, take State Road 1008 north approximately 5 miles.

Kerr Lake

Vance County (Bullocksville): 3.5 miles west of Drewry on State Road 1366.

Vance County (Henderson Point): 2 miles north of Townsville on N.C. 39 to State Road 1356, 2.5 miles to State Road 1359, 1.4 miles to the area.

Vance County (Hibernia): 1.2 miles north of Townsville on N.C. 39 to State Road 1347, 2.1 miles to the area.

Warren County (county line): 3 miles north of Drewry on State Road 1200 to State Road 1202, then .75 miles to State Road 1361, then 1.2 miles to State Road 1242, then .5 miles to the area.

Warren County (Kimball Point): 5 miles north of Drewry on State Road 1200 to State Road 1204, 1.5 miles to area.

Kitty Hawk Bay

Dare County (Avalon Beach): At Avalon Beach, .5 miles west of U.S. 158.

Little River
Pasquotank County (Hall's Creek): Between Nixonton and U.S. 17 on State Road 1140.

Lookout Shoals Lake
Catawba County (Lookout Shoals): Near Lookout Dam, 6 miles northeast of Conover on State Road 1006 off N.C. 16.

Lumber River
Hoke County (Wagram): On U.S. 401 approximately 1 mile northeast of Wagram.
Robeson County (High Hill): at the south edge of Lumberton on U.S. 74 (Business) at the Lumber River Bridge.
Robeson County (McNeil's Bridge): From U.S. 301 Bypass, take N.C. 72 northwest to the area (within sight of U.S. 301).

Meherrin River
Hertford County (Murfreesboro): North side of bridge on U.S. 258 at Murfreesboro.

Mayo Reservoir
Person County (Triple Spring): Approximately 9 miles north of Roxboro on N.C. 42, turn west on State Road 1515, go 1 mile to the area.

Mountain Island Lake
Gaston County (River Bend): 12 miles northwest of Charlotte on N.C. 16 to State Road 1912, then north .3 miles to the access area road.
Mecklenburg County (Davidson Creek): Northwest of Charlotte, 12 miles on State Road 2074 (Beatties Ford), turn left on State Road 2165.

Nantahala Lake
Macon County (Choga Creek): East of Andrews via State
Road 1505 and U.S. Forest Service Road 30.
Macon County (Rocky Branch): 19 miles west of Franklin via
U.S. 64 and State Road 1310.

Neuse River
Craven County (Bridgeton): 1 miles north of Bridgeton just
off U.S. 17.
Johnston County (Richardson's Bridge): Off State Road 1201,
approximately 9 miles southeast of Smithfield.
Lenoir County (Kinston): On U.S. 70 west in Kinston, adja-
cent to the Neuse River Bridge.
Wayne County (Goldsboro): Adjacent to U.S. 117 south of
Goldsboro.
Wayne County (Cox's Ferry): On Wayne County Road 1224
approximately 9 miles west of Goldsboro.
Wayne County (Seven Springs): Adjacent to the highway
bridge on State Road 1731 in Seven Springs.

New River
Onslow County (Jacksonville): Adjacent to the U.S. 17 New
River Bridge in Jacksonville.

Northeast Cape Fear River
Duplin County (Kenansville): Between Kenansville and
Beulaville on N.C. 24.
New Hanover County (Castle Hayne): Adjacent to the U.S.
117 bridge over the Northeast Cape Fear River.
Pender County (Holly Shelter): At Holly Shelter Refuge, 6
miles south of N.C. 53 via State Road 1523 and 1520.
Pender County (Sawpit Landing): On N.C. 53, 3 miles north
of Burgaw, turn on State Road 1512. The launching area is at
the end of State Road 1512.

Pamlico River
Beaufort County (Smith's Creek): In the Goose Creek Game
Land area on N.C. 33, approximately 2 miles west of
Hobucken.

Pamlico Sound
Dare County (Stumpy Point): At the end of State Road 1100.
Hyde County (Engelhard): East of U.S. 264 at the north town
limits of Engelhard.

Pasquotank River
Pasquotank County (Elizabeth City): From Elizabeth City,
take U.S. 17 north to Knobb Creek Road approximately .5
miles to the area.

Pee Dee River
Anson County (Red Hill): 8 miles north of Wadesboro on
N.C. 109.
Richmond County (Blewett): From Rockingham, approxi-
mately 4 miles west on U.S. 74 to State Road 1140, 1 mile to
State Road 1141, approximately 3.5 miles to the area.
Richmond County (Rockingham): On U.S. 74, approximately
6 miles west of Rockingham.

Perquimans River
Perquimans County (Perquimans): From Hertford, east on
State Road 1300, approximately 9 miles to State Road 1319,
then 1 mile to the area.

Rhodhiss Lake
Burke County (Johns's River): 3.8 miles north of Morganton
on N.C. 18.
Caldwell County (Castle Bridge): North of Connelly Springs
at Castle Bridge via State Road 1001.

Caldwell County (Dry Pond): 1 mile southwest of Granite Falls.
Caldwell County (Tater Hole): Approximately .75 miles from the post office on Lakeside Avenue in Granite Falls.

Roanoke Rapids Lake

Halifax County (Thelma): 2 miles northeast of Thelma via State Road 1400 and 1422.
Northampton County (Vultare): Take N.C. 46 to Vultare, then south to State Road 1213 and go to the end of the road.

Roanoke River

Halifax County (Edwards Ferry): From Scotland Neck take U.S. 258 north, approximately 5 miles to the river bridge.
Halifax County (Weldon): On U.S. 301 at Weldon.
Martin County (Hamilton): In the town limits of Hamilton.
Martin County (Williamston): Located adjacent to the Roanoke River bridge on U.S. 17 at Williamston.
Northampton County (Gaston): At the northwest end of the N.C. 48 bridge north of Roanoke Rapids.
Washington County (Plymouth): Adjacent to the N.C. 45 bridge east of Plymouth.

Salters Creek

Carteret County (Salters Creek): From Beaufort, go east on U.S. 70 toward Cedar Island. The area is at the northeast end of the high-rise bridge that crosses Nelson Bay.

Santeetlah Lake

Graham County (Avey Creek): 11 miles west of Robbinsville. Turn left on the Forest Service Road approximately 5 miles to the area.
Graham County (Ranger Station): 5 miles west of Robbinsville on State Road 1127.

Scuppernong River
Tyrrell County (Columbia): 1 mile west of Columbia off U.S. 64.

Shearon Harris Reservoir
Chatham County (dam site): From N.C. 42 at Corinth, take State Road 1912 north to the junction of State Road 1914, and follow State Road 1914 to the area on the right.
Wake County (Hollman's Crossing): From Raleigh, travel west on U.S. 1 to the New Hill exit. Exit onto State Road 1127, go south to State Road 1130, and follow State Road 1130 west of the access area.

Shelter Creek
Pender County (Shelter Creek): 9 miles east of Burgaw, .25 miles off N.C. 53, on State Road 1523.

Smith's Creek
Pamlico County (Oriental): At the end of Midgette Street, in the town limits on the west side of the N.C. 55 bridge.

South River
Bladen County (Ennis Bridge): From N.C. 210, 5 miles south of N.C. 41, take State Road 1007 1 mile east to the area.
Bladen County (Sloan's Bridge): 2 miles southwest of Garland on U.S. 701.

South Yadkin River
Davie County (Cooleemee): 2 miles north of Cooleemee on State Road 1116 (Davie Academy Road).

Tar River
Edgecombe County (Bell's Bridge): 1 mile north of Tarboro on N.C. 44 at Bell's bridge.

Edgecombe County (Old Sparta): On N.C. 42 at Old Sparta.
Pitt County (Falkland): On State Road 1400, off N.C. 43, 1 mile east of Falkland.
Pitt County (Greenville): Off N.C. 33 approximately 1 mile east of the city limits of Greenville, turn north on State Road 1533, approximately .5 miles to the area.

Taylor's Creek
Carteret County (Taylor's Creek, Beaufort): From Beaufort, take U.S. 70 east to State Road 1310, turn right, and go to State Road 1312; turn right and go 100 yards to the area.

Lake Tillery
Montgomery County (Lilly's Bridge): 5 miles west of Mt. Gilead. Take N.C. 731, turn right on State Road 1110.
Montgomery County (Swift Island): 5 miles southeast of Albemarle on N.C. 27-73.
Stanly County (Norwood): From Norwood, take State Road 1740 approximately 1 mile to the area.
Stanly County (Stony Mountain) From Albemarle, east on N.C. 24, 27, and 73 approximately 5 miles to the Lighthouse Marina Road. The site is adjacent to the marina.

Tuckertown Lake
Davidson County (High Rock): On Davidson County Road 1002 approximately 4 miles west of Healing Springs.
Rowan County (Flat Creek): On State Road 2148, 3 miles north of N.C. 49 via State Road 2152.

Waccamaw Lake
Columbus County (Lake Waccamaw): On Lake Shore Road west of N.C. 214.
Columbus County (Big Creek): Northeast shore of Lake Waccamaw on State Road 1947.

Waccamaw River

Brunswick County (Waccamaw River): Adjacent to the N.C. 904 Bridge across the Waccamaw River in Brunswick County.

White Oak River

Jones County (Haywood's Landing): 5 miles southeast of Maysville, south of N.C. 58.

Wolf Creek Lake

Jackson County (Wolf Creek): 5.1 miles east of Tuckasegee of N.C. 281 approximately 5 miles from the end of the pavement.

Yadkin River

Davie County (Concord Church): From Fork, on U.S. 64, go west 4 miles on N.C. 801 to the access road leading southeast, then go .5 miles to the area.

Appendix B

The Artificial Worm

There is no doubt about it: The artificial worm is by far the most popular lure among bass anglers in North Carolina, a position it has enjoyed for many years and probably will continue to enjoy for many years to come.

I remember the first time I ever saw anybody catch a bass on an artificial worm. It was about 1952, and I had been home only a few weeks from Korea after having served in the "police action."

Richard "Butch" Phillips and I went out on Lake Wylie. Butch said he had a new type of lure. It was an artificial worm with three hooks in it. As I recall, Butch fished the worm below several split shots.

He cast out over a point, let the worm settle, and then reeled it in slowly. When he got a tap, he followed the usual practice of the day: he let the bass run a long way and then set the hook. He caught three or four bass in a short time, as I recall. He talked me into trying the worm. I did, but I didn't catch any fish; I didn't know how to use it properly.

Anglers now fish the worm differently than the way we did in those days, but it's still just as deadly, or perhaps more so. In some areas of the country, including North Carolina, it probably catches more fish than all other lures combined.

Nowadays, most experts prefer to use the "Texas rig" method of inserting the hook into the worm. This, along with a bullet weight, makes the worm semi-weedless and semi-snagless. The "South Carolina rig" is the second-most popular method of rigging the worm. It is especially useful when you want to fish the worm just off the bottom. (See the accompanying illustration if you don't know how to rig a worm.)

I remember when two friends, Bill Black and Taylor Turner,

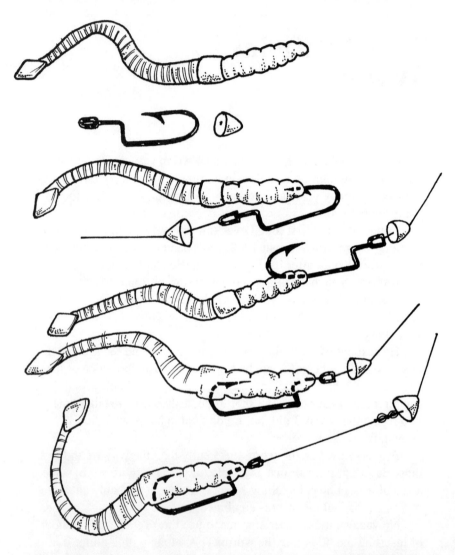

Drawings by Kaye Florance

To rig an artificial worm "Texas style," follow these steps (from top to bottom). First, insert the hook in the worm a fraction of inch, then turn the hook and bring it out of the side of the worm. Finally, bury the barb of the hook in the worm. The bottom illustration shows a worm rigged "South Carolina style." The South Carolina rig resembles the Texas rig, but a swivel is placed on the line about ten inches above the worm. This prevents the sliding sinker from sliding down to the worm, allowing the worm to float off the bottom.

caught as many bass as I have ever seen anybody catch on the Pungo River. They both were using artificial worms. I told Taylor I couldn't figure out why I lost so many bass when I used a worm.

"You don't set the hook hard enough," Taylor said.

He and Bill showed me how to drop my rod as soon as I felt a tap, reel in the slack, and then snap the rod back. They said I should set the hook when I felt even a nudge.

I followed his advice and lost fewer fish.

Some people still rig the worm the old way. This style of worm usually has three weedless hooks.

Some of the largest bass I ever saw one person catch in one day on Currituck Sound were caught on the old-fashioned worm and fished the old-fashioned way. The bass were caught by Paul Talbert, a professional airplane pilot. He let the bass run awhile before setting the hook, just like Butch Phillips did the first time I ever saw anybody fish with an artificial worm. It's hard to argue with success.

Appendix C

All The Lures You Need

Most of us possess so many fishing lures that you'd think we were all wealthy and the lures were tax-deductible. We are suckers for almost any new lure that comes out, no matter how ridiculous in appearance. In my lifetime, I have owned everything from a spinner lure with a mother-of-pearl blade to gold-plated spoons to a lure you inserted Alka-Seltzer tablets into so it would fizz.

But over the years, I have conducted an informal, unscientific poll among the skilled anglers I've met. I concluded that we really need only eight lures to fish for freshwater bass from the mountains to the coast.

What are these lures?

It shouldn't surprise anybody to learn that the artificial worm is the Number 1 lure among North Carolina anglers. The worm apparently appeals to bass because it is life-like. It can be rigged so it's semi-weedless. And it is versatile. It can be fished as a topwater bait if you use it without a weight. It can be fished shallow if you use it with a light sinker. Or it can be fished on the deep bottom if you use a heavy sinker.

The lure mentioned the second most often was no surprise, either: the spinner bait. Again, one reason it is so effective is that it's versatile. It, too, can be fished at almost any depth. It can be fished deep by fishing it slowly. With a faster retrieve, it runs shallow. Or it will come right up to the top if you retrieve it very fast. It is also semi-weedless.

The lure mentioned the third most often by the good anglers I talked to surprised me: It is the thin minnow, a shallow-running lure such as the Rapala, Rebel, Bang-O-Lure, or any others of the same family.

The fourth most popular lure among North Carolina anglers is a deep-diving bait, a lure now known as a "crankbait."

Another lure you'd need to fish all of North Carolina, of course, is a topwater lure. I would probably choose a lure that has propellers on either the rear or on both the front and rear.

Another lure listed frequently by successful anglers is the jigging-type lure, such as the lead-bodied lures with a spinner on the back or a deep jigging spoon.

And just because I enjoy fishing eastern North Carolina waters so much, I would choose a Johnson weedless spoon, probably silver.

The eighth lure that good anglers mention the most often is the weedless jig with a rubber tail designed to be used with pork or a soft plastic trailer.

So there you have it. You can buy those eight lures and send your son or daughter to Harvard with the money you'd normally spend on lures.

Index

Oregon Inlet, 62
Orvis fly-fishing course, 183
Osborne, Tommy, 169-173
Outer Banks, 35, 60, 64, 75, 85, 180, 209
Owens, Johnny, 61
Oxford, N.C., 135

P

Page, Hugh, 74
Pamlico River, 22, 95-96
Panhandle, 134
Pantego Creek, 91-92
Panther Martin lure, 171
Pasquotank River, 35-41, 191
Paysour, Buck, 88, 209
Paysour, Conrad, 14, 112, 136, 153-154
Paysour, Doris Dale, 7, 61, 90, 108, 139, 151, 157, 179
Paysour, John Gerard, 70
Pea Hill, 134
Peck's Popper lure, 163
Pee Dee River, 121, 124-126
Peeler, John, 108
Pennsylvania, 36, 51, 69, 139, 212-213
Perquimans River, 49
Perry, L.E. "Buck," 9, 195-200
Perry, Walt, 77
Perry, Warner, 46-49
Peterson, John, 1, 23, 30, 51, 89
Pflueger Chum spoon, 14
Phelps Lake, 56
Piedmont region, 6, 16, 24, 75, 101-103, 117, 203
Piedmont Triad International Airport, 204
Piney Island Club, 178
Pittsboro, N.C., 102, 138, 142

plastic worms, 6, 25-26, 30, 38, 40, 47, 55, 68, 91, 107, 112, 125, 197
plugs, 46, 121, 125, 131, 135, 154, 189
popping bug lures, 2-3, 24, 39, 47, 55, 59, 63, 66, 69-70, 74, 89, 96, 153, 163, 177-180, 182-184
Pungo Creek, 1-2, 89-90, 92-94
Pungo Lake, 56
Pungo River, 13, 17, 87-96
puppy drum, 87-88, 90

Q

Queen Anne's Creek, 48

R

Rainey, Mike, 114
Raleigh, N.C., 9, 101-102, 142-143, 167, 185
Rapala lure, 1-2, 30, 37-38, 45, 50, 54-55, 83, 89, 91, 97, 122, 124, 132, 153-154, 200-201
Reagan, Ronald, 69, 183, 213
Rebel lure, 25, 30, 37-38, 45-46, 50, 54, 83, 89-91, 97, 121-122, 132, 153-154, 207
redbreast sunfish, 29
Reece, Kemp Jr., 14-15
Reece, Kemp Sr., 14
Reeves, Henry, 90
Reid, Charlie, 69
Rhodhiss Lake, 105, 109-110
Rich, Hugh, 21
Ricketson, Tom, 64
riprap, 138, 165